Contents

INTRODUCTION

Pápalo. That was the herb that got me started on my hydroponic journey. Back in 2015 while I was visiting Los Angeles, my friend Sean had me taste a leaf from the farmers' market in Santa Monica. It was small and flat and tasted like cilantro with an extra hint of citrus freshness, which makes it perfect for use in Mexican *cemitas* and other *tortas* and tacos. You can sometimes find it in California, and certainly in Mexico, but it's nearly impossible to source anywhere else, especially in large cities like New York, where I was about to move. I was intrigued.

I had been living in Japan for eight years, an experience that instilled in me an eternal respect for fresh ingredients and the detail and care that goes into sourcing them. If you've been lucky enough to visit a grocery store in Japan, you'll see how meticulously the Japanese package their fruits and vegetables, not to mention grow and harvest them. Where to get the best apples, peaches, and strawberries is still very much common knowledge throughout the country. That kind of knowledge exists all over the world, but we need to be careful to preserve and practice it in places where mass production has often obliterated seasonality and common sense in choosing the correct produce at the correct time of year.

It was an exciting thought: all over the world amazing flavors are packed in little-known herbs and obscure vegetables, but they're only available for a few weeks a year in very limited locations. What if there was a way to bring those ingredients to New York City year-round, without compromising their quality?

I'd read a few news stories about Japanese companies growing lettuce under LED lights in repurposed semiconductor factories. All these companies were using something called hydroponics—a method of growing plants in water instead of soil. But all I knew about hydroponics was that people used it to grow marijuana in their basements. Employing it for a different purpose never occurred to me—until then. I couldn't get the idea of growing fresh pápalo and other exotic edible plants out of my head. Maybe I could do this. In New York. With exotic ingredients. With hydroponics.

I began researching hydroponic farming and what it would take to make it work. The information available was sparse, confusing, and mostly focused on growing marijuana. But when I met David Goldstein, a hydroponics expert who would soon become the head horticulturalist in my new business, I was ready to take the plunge and start an indoor hydroponic farm for growing rare herbs, edible flowers, and microgreens.

Many people have heard of hydroponic farming but have never seen its inner workings up close or really understood it. It sounds complicated and science-y. The knowledge and the equipment necessary have come of age only in the last few years, and much of the gear looks like something out of a science-fiction movie. Most of the existing information is either for people secretly growing weed in a cellar or for large-scale industrial farms with huge, complex systems. Hydroponic terminology can be confusing, and you can spend hours watching how-to videos online, only to feel like you know even less than when you started. But the basic principles are simple to understand, and you'll be surprised at how easy it is to try at home with some simple materials and brief instructions. This book is my way of sharing hydroponics and some of the weird and wonderful culinary plants that David and I grow at Farm.One.

OUR FARM

The air is warm and humid. We light our plants with LEDs, which cast a pinkish-purply glow. Pumps whir and drone on and off at intervals. This is our hydroponic system. Smells come and go, most of them pleasant herbal aromas that merge into a minty-anisey-grassy background bouquet. Occasionally you'll catch a whiff of a sharper perfume, like that of funky fish mint or the intoxicating Aztec sweet herb—or something more disagreeable, like sprouting peas. Oscillating fans hum and spread a choppy breeze, so these odors come and go. If you close your eyes, the watery sounds and smells might even convince you that you're on a boat drifting lazily down a remote jungle river.

At Farm.One, we grow exotic, high-end herbs, edible flowers, and microgreens for the best chefs in New York City. Our facilities are relatively tiny and amount to the size of a city apartment: the one at the Institute of Culinary Education (ICE) in Lower Manhattan is just three hundred square feet, and the one in Tribeca is twelve hundred square feet. We focus on rarity and flavor, use no pesticides or other chemicals, and everything we grow is clean enough to eat as soon as it's picked. We harvest and deliver on the same day, using bikes and the subway, so if an order is placed by ten o'clock in the morning, we get it to the restaurant by five o'clock in the afternoon. The produce is packed in reusable containers, which we pick up from our customers the next time we deliver. A typical order might be for a pound of red shiso, fifty violas, or a tray of micro bronze fennel that a chef will use to garnish dozens of dishes. We're trying to grow things that most people have never tasted or had access to, and we're growing them in a controlled environment that allows them to be properly cared for. No one else in New York is doing that.

Before we started Farm.One, I was worried that hydroponically raised plants might taste dull and antiseptic. Hydroponics had a reputation for bland, tasteless produce, probably because we have this mistaken idea that plants sitting in water will somehow become watery—that the water will "soak" into them, diluting their flavor. This is completely wrong. The variety of seeds you choose and how you care for them influence flavor far more than the growing method does. Well-grown hydroponic herbs have powerful, bold, impressive flavor. Now, just a year into the farm's existence, some of the best chefs in the world—César Ramirez (of the Chef's Table at Brooklyn Fare), and Ronny Emborg (of Atera), Daniel Boulud (of Daniel and many others), and Jung Sik Yim (Jungsik)—use our products, such as purple oxalis, anise hyssop, and fennel crowns, every day. Hydroponics work!

WORKING WITH CHEFS

Taking samples to a new restaurant client can be a bit daunting. Normally the service entrance is nondescript, worn and scuffed, and opens onto a side alleyway. Sometimes it's labeled, but often it's not. You knock and most of the time there is no answer because everyone's too busy to hear it. So you just open the door and poke your head inside. Although it seems strange and unnerving to enter the chef's domain the first few times, after a while you realize that chefs love to sample new produce. Bringing around fresh herbs grown just a few minutes away is a gift warmly welcomed.

Great chefs can make the decision on what to buy in just a few seconds. When something tastes good, they recognize it right away. When it goes well, this is one of the most pleasurable sales experiences around. Seeing Farm.One's product turn up on a menu the next day (often through a random tourist's Instagram feed) is also really fun. Most of the time the farm's products are used as part of the garnish or presentation, so the view of them on the plate is often very good. What we sell varies by the season, and the summertime sees much more demand for flowers and other summery products. But we can grow the same product year-round, so it's much more about what a chef wants for a menu than sticking closely to a season or a trend.

Sometimes a product is crazily popular for a few months (in 2016 it was red-veined sorrel), and then even "banned" in some kitchens because of its overuse. But most of the time chefs have a particular favorite—an herb or flower that he or she is looking for. And they won't compromise on the flavor.

ABOUT THIS BOOK

In this book, I'll break down some of the simple principles of hydroponics that have been developed over the past few hundred years. I'll tell you how to start growing hydroponic plants at home, look after them, and harvest what you grow. Herbs, leafy greens, microgreens, and flowers will be our primary focus, but you can grow almost anything hydroponically, like potatoes, cucumbers, tomatoes, fruits such as strawberries and blueberries, and even ornamental plants. I'm also looking forward to introducing you to a number of unusual culinary plants (see page 74), all of which can be grown in a simple hydroponic system. These exotic varieties often have flavors and aromas you've never come across before.

One of the advantages of growing unusual plants at home is that it dramatically increases the range of ingredients available to you, broadening your horizons as a cook. To give you confidence in your experimentation, I've included some flavor pairings and straightforward "non-recipes" to show you how easy it can be to use these plants in your kitchen. You'll find those with each plant profile in Chapter 3.

Once you get started, you'll quickly see that hydroponics can be a fun, hassle-free way to grow some amazing things at home.

CHAPTER ONE

Why Hydroponics?

Our planet's megacities bring together multiple cultures, attract tourists from all over the globe, host a wild array of entertainments, and combine countless trends in one place. With that comes diversity of foods, ingredients, and influences. Our range of food options now is orders of magnitude greater than what was available when we were children.

If I think back to my parents' generation in the United Kingdom, having an Indian meal was seen as adventurous. But now, "exotic" cuisines like Japanese, Mexican, Italian, and Chinese are offered virtually everywhere. Over the next few years, we will see experimental fine dining coming from some of the more remote corners of the world, and in the near future, I wouldn't be surprised if Michelin stars and other accolades start going to more Cambodian, Nepalese, Kazakh, Moroccan, or Ethiopian chefs. That kind of attention could mean more people becoming interested in trying those cuisines. With the introduction of new foods comes an appreciation of different flavor profiles and a need for different herbs and ingredients in every city of the world. But therein lies a problem: how do we make these specialized ingredients available globally?

Seasonal food is prized mainly because seasonal means local and local means fresh. This is because the natural growing seasons for plants depend on the climate. So a great chef can stay seasonal and make a fantastic dessert in February using winter fruits and other cold-weather produce. But we demand more. We want to enjoy the flavors of spring greens, ripe summer fruits, and fresh herbs year-round. While it's true that few of us crave a cold green salad in January or a hot soup on a summer day, we expect to be able to get almost anything, any time of year, anywhere. For example, we expect to be able to eat South American herbs in August in Jakarta. That usually requires shipping that exotic produce halfway around the world and then keeping it in cold storage to forestall its demise before it hits the plate. Or even worse, it means growing varieties that are selected for their high yield, slow aging, and resistance to pests rather than for their flavor. This has led to a massive decline in the quality and flavor of much of the produce available in grocery stores: tomatoes, for example, are more often designed to look aesthetically pleasing than to taste great, and apples are bred for their ability to sit on a shelf without spoiling.

Instead of this reversion to boring, commercialized produce that has sat on a truck for days, we can now grow them anywhere, whatever the time of year, with hydroponics. We can pick leaves and have them on a plate within minutes or hours. And we can grow varieties with true flavor. They are not the most disease-resistant or the most beautiful, but they are the tastiest.

Skeptics who say, "Isn't this an unnatural way to cut seasonality completely out of the equation?" need to think about it differently. A modern subway is an unnatural thing; so is a text message and a phone that you can carry around with you. But these advances in technology also connect us, they give our cities life, they keep friends in touch, and they bridge cultures, so we embrace them. Over the coming decades, we will all be using new ways to grow fresh, abundant, beautiful plants in urban areas, and we will start to embrace the technologies that make that possible in the same way we have welcomed the mobile phone.

Sixty years ago, the biggest question in the food industry was, how are we going to feed our growing world population? Fast-forward to today and the questions we have about food are far more complex and nuanced. We have created huge monoculture farms that produce more food than is necessary, but they are thousands of miles away from the people who consume the food. They produce just a handful of crops, such as wheat, soy, corn, potatoes, and rice. Even leafy greens come in remarkably little variety.

In solving the problem of growing enough food, we have created dozens of others. Rain forest destruction, widespread pesticide use, obesity and all the diseases related to it, factory farming, food miles, drought, and other issues are now becoming pressing problems for humanity as a whole. And in the developed nations, where over 74 percent of the population now lives in cities, access to personal green space like a backyard is rare. That means we are less and less able to grow our own food.

We need to find solutions to these new problems. Hydroponics is an efficient option for growing fresh produce in cities, as it is a clean, contained technology that allows year-round cultivation without the need for soil. Whether done on a large scale in a vertical farm or on a windowsill, it gives us all a fresh, new opportunity to grow what we eat.

Hydroponics is incredibly water-efficient compared to traditional growing, making it an obvious choice for the cities of the future where access to fresh water will likely become even more restricted. Growing in the city dramatically reduces food miles, our food's carbon footprint, and food waste. And growing indoors dramatically reduces or eliminates pesticide use, making food safer for the person who grows it and the person who eats it. Growing hydroponically at home makes sense now, and I guarantee that in ten years' time it will be remarkably more common.

THE HISTORY OF HYDROPONICS

As I was learning about hydroponics before starting Farm.One, I often came across misleading information implying that the technique was hundreds or even thousands of years old—probably to make people more comfortable with the idea of growing plants without soil. But the more I researched, the more it became clear that the successful hydroponics of today required the hard work and ingenuity of a long line of biologists and other scientists determined first to find out how plants work and then how to reverse-engineer the system of plant nutrition. That could not have been done effectively even two hundred years ago.

For modern hydroponics to emerge, we needed a good understanding of what a plant needs in order to survive—water, carbon dioxide, oxygen in the root zone, the right combination of mineral nutrients, light—and the technology to manage those factors reliably throughout the plant's life cycle. Our progress toward that knowledge has happened mostly within the last four hundred years, though a couple of precursors are interesting and might have been inspirational. For example, the hanging gardens of Babylon are sometimes cited as an early example of soil-free, or hydroponic, agriculture. If these gardens actually existed, they were more likely a set of raised soil beds, irrigated through intensive manual labor, which, though an impressive feat, is not quite hydroponics.

CHINAMPAS

Chinampa, a type of agriculture created by the Aztecs for growing crops on shallow lake beds in the Valley of Mexico, is often credited as a step toward developing hydroponics. A *chinampa* is a kind of mini artificial island built by piling up soil from a shallow lake bed until it breaks the surface and forms a flat growing area surrounded by water. The first *chinampas* date from the fifteenth century and seem to have ranged in size from about thirty by ten feet to three hundred by thirty feet.

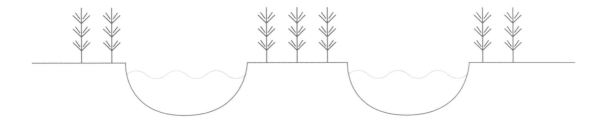

Clearly, the *chinampa* design is not a true hydroponic system, as the plants still grow in soil. But these artificial islands had a key advantage in that their beds were surrounded by flooded channels, which gave plants continuous access to lake water and created the potential for reliable growth independent of rainfall. By scraping sediment from the bottom of the lakes to replenish the topsoil, farmers were also taking advantage of the nutrients from fish waste, creating a rudimentary form of aquaponics—a form of hydroponics that uses the waste of aquatic animals as plant food.

THE WILLOW TREE EXPERIMENT

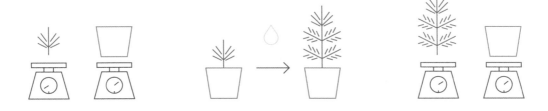

In 1634, Jan Baptist van Helmont, a Flemish scientist known for identifying carbon dioxide gas, was put under house arrest by agents of the Spanish Inquisition. His crime? Studying plants and other natural phenomena. Undaunted by his confinement, Van Helmont was curious about the current assumption of his time that plants "eat" soil to grow, so he secretly conducted a now-famous plant experiment at his home to test this theory. He planted a young willow tree in a large pot full of roughly two hundred pounds of soil and then gave it nothing but water for five years. By this point, the tree had grown to a weight of around 169 pounds, while the soil had decreased in mass by only about two ounces. Van Helmont's conclusion was that plants build their mass from water, not soil. While this conclusion was faulty (and glaringly omitted carbon dioxide), it was a key step in showing that soil is not essential to plant growth.

MINT IN WATER

In his 1661 book *The Sceptical Chymist*, Robert Boyle described a simple experiment in water:

> I took a top of spearmint, about an inch long, and put it into a good phial full of spring water, so as the upper part of the mint was above the neck of the glass, and the lower part immersed in the water; within a few days this mint began to shoot forth roots into the water, and to display its leaves, and aspire upwards; and in a short time it had numerous roots and leaves, and these very strong and fragrant of the odour of the mint; but the heat of my chamber, as I suppose, killed the plant, when it was grown to have a pretty thick stalk, which with the various and ramified roots, which it shot into the water as if it had been earth, presented in the transparent flower-pot a spectacle not unpleasant to behold.

Later in the same book, Boyle describes Van Helmont's willow tree experiment—they were both clearly intrigued by some of the same plant-life mysteries.

In his 1699 article "Some Thoughts and Experiments Concerning Vegetation," John Woodward published the results of his "water culture" experiments, which he had performed in 1691 by putting cuttings of mint and other plants into covered glass vials. He tested the weight of the plants before and after several months of growth and found that plants in water from the River Thames and from springs grew better than plants in distilled water. We know now that the minerals dissolved in the river and spring water were providing some nutrition to the plants, while the distilled water was devoid of impurities. In 1772, in his book *Experiments and Observations on Different Kinds of Air*, Joseph Priestley followed this research with his own discovery that over time a mint plant (clearly a popular plant to experiment with) could somehow replenish the oxygen in a sealed chamber.

Van Helmont, Boyle, Woodward, and Priestley were all building useful knowledge about plant physiology. In the 1770s, another contributor, the Dutch biologist Jan Ingenhousz, after a meeting with Priestley, observed the gas bubbles produced when submerged plants were exposed to sunlight. He later concluded this gas was oxygen, thus identifying the basic elements of photosynthesis. But it would take more than seventy years for the next key step: understanding the full process of photosynthesis and the mineral requirements of plants.

THE FIRST NUTRIENT SOLUTION

Between 1856 and 1874, Julius von Sachs, a prominent German botanist, made a series of rapid discoveries about plant biology, especially about the movement of water in plants, the role of roots, and the role of starch and carbon dioxide in photosynthesis. He ventured a first guess about the minimal nutrient solution (see page 22) required for the growth of plants, using a mix of potassium, nitrogen, phosphorus, calcium, sulfur, sodium, chloride, magnesium, and iron in experiments with plants suspended in a nutrient solution.

In the late 1920s, William Gericke at the University of California, Berkeley, used the word *hydroponics* for the first time in reference to the growing of plants in water. The term is made up of the Greek *hydro*, or "water," and *ponos*, or "work."

In 1938, also at UC Berkeley, Dennis Hoagland and Daniel Arnon published a study about a twelve-part nutrient solution that refined Sachs's original approach, providing a more complete set of nutrients for plants. This recipe was so effective that it became the basis for many future hydroponic nutrient solutions, revised and added to by thousands of scientists and home growers. This period produced even more innovation, as the 1940s also saw the development of the first flood and drain hydroponic systems (see page 26).

THE FIRST HYDROPONIC FARMS

By the end of World War II, the logistics of supplying fresh vegetables to the US military stationed on remote islands around the world had become difficult and sometimes impossible. Ascension Island, an isolated and nearly barren volcanic island near the equator in the south Atlantic Ocean, became home to one of the first large hydroponic farms. The farm, which used long water channels filled with volcanic rock as a growing substrate, was successful, and soon other large hydroponic facilities were set up on the islands of Iwo Jima, Okinawa, and Wake near Hawaii, as well as inland in Iraq and Bahrain. By 1952, some eight million pounds of fresh produce were being grown for the military on hydroponic farms.

This use of volcanic rock did not go unnoticed by Hawaiian cannabis growers, who started to use similar materials in rudimentary home hydroponic systems. Today, perlite and pumice are used by hydroponic growers of all kinds, along with other materials that mimic the porosity of volcanic rocks.

Throughout the 1960s and 1970s, techniques and materials continued to be refined, including the development of the nutrient film technique in the United Kingdom, drip irrigation systems at New York's Cornell University, the aeroponic method in Italy, and rockwool as a growing medium in the Netherlands.

The general public's first introduction to the world of hydroponics came in 1982, when The Land pavilion at the EPCOT Center at Florida's Walt Disney World introduced a journey through greenhouses that house a futuristic hydroponic garden. Interestingly, these greenhouses grow produce for Disney World's restaurants and show off some of the most unusual and creative uses of the growing system.

A little more than a decade later, a new kind of basic hydroponic system was developed by Bernard A. Kratky, a horticulturalist at the University of Hawaii. His first paper on his discovery described it as "a capillary, noncirculating hydroponic method for leaf and semi-head lettuce." It is a wonderfully simple setup that requires no electricity or pumps, which makes it both easy and cheap (see page 28 for more on the Kratky systems).

The past decade has seen rapid innovation, with companies continually improving on some of these first hydroponic systems. As LED lighting has become more affordable, both home and commercial growers have also started to use artificial lighting, either to boost production in winter months or as their only light source.

What's next? Probably more and more automation. While hydroponic plumbing components have been automated with simple timers for years, engineers are working on artificial intelligence systems (such as computer vision software that can detect unhealthy leaves), augmented reality that allows growers to view crop performance in the field just by looking, and even robots for harvesting. But don't worry: for the home hydroponic grower, things can stay very simple!

ESSENTIAL TERMINOLOGY

Hydroponics means growing plants in a water-nutrient solution rather than soil. Lots of technical terms are involved. Here are some of the key ones.

Aeroponics is a variation of hydroponics in which a fine mist of nutrient solution is sprayed onto a plant's roots.

Aquaponics is a popular variant of hydroponics in which the excretions of fish or other aquatic life are used to create nutrients for plants in a hydroponic system.

Coconut husk is a hydroponic growing medium made of recycled coconut (coco) husks, or sometimes a mixture of coconut husks and perlite (a naturally occurring volcanic glass).

Cotyledon is the first set of leaves to emerge from a sprouted seed. These leaves are also sometimes called "baby leaves," which can be confusing in a culinary setting.

Daily light integral (DLI) is the overall amount of light received by a plant in a day. It is made up of the intensity of the light combined with the number of hours the light is received by the plant.

Deep water culture (DWC) is a simple hydroponic system made up of a deep tray filled with an aerated nutrient solution, normally with rafts floating on top where the plants sit.

A **Dutch bucket** is an easily scaled hydroponic system made up of buckets filled with a hydroponic growing medium, with inflows of a nutrient solution and outflows of wastewater.

Electrical conductivity (EC) is a method of measuring the level of dissolved mineral solids in a liquid. It is a popular way to test the concentration of nutrient solutions used in hydroponics.

A **flood and drain system** uses pumps, normally on a timer, to periodically flood a growing tray with a nutrient solution.

A garden tray is a plastic tray, typically black, used for holding the growing medium and the growing plants.

A growing medium is a soil-like substance used in a hydroponic system to support a plant. It is normally inert, providing no nutrition, just structure.

Kratky is a type of hydroponic system in which the plant is suspended above a nutrient solution reservoir. As the plant grows and consumes water from the roots, reducing the water level, an air gap is created that provides the roots oxygen.

Nutrient film technique (NFT) is a hydroponic system that uses a central reservoir from which nutrients are pumped up and trickled down channels in a thin layer, or "film."

A nutrient solution is a mixture of minerals (and sometimes other components such as fungi and bacteria) that provides food for the plants in a hydroponic system.

pH is a measure of the acidity or alkalinity of a substance. A pH under 7.0 is acidic and a pH over 7.0 is alkaline.

A plant variety is a specific type of plant within a species. Often, dramatically different-tasting herbs are members of the same species, so "variety" is used to distinguish the fellow species members from one another.

Rockwool is a hydroponic growing medium made of heat-treated stone and clay. It is available in cubes for planting full plants and in flat sheets for raising microgreens.

Terpenes are particular types of oil-based volatile compounds found in many plants. Plants may use them to attract and repel different kinds of insects and animals—just as they are used between types of insects as an attractor and repellent.

Vertical farming is so called because of the stacked growing levels made possible by using an artificial light source rather than the sun. Most vertical farms are hydroponic.

Volatile flavor compounds are chemical compounds that are transported through the air to the nose for us to smell. The term is often used to refer to the particular aroma of culinary herbs.

CORE HYDROPONIC PRINCIPLES

Before we get further into explaining the principles of hydroponics, let's review some basics about how plants work.

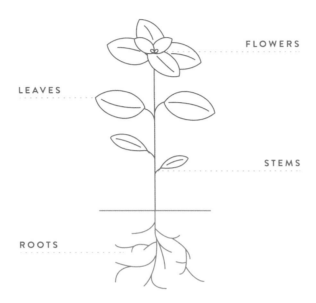

Roots absorb water and minerals from the soil or whatever growing medium is used. They are covered with small hairs that help add more area through which absorption can happen. Roots also anchor the plant and store extra food for future use.

Stems provide support for the plant. They also transport water and nutrients from the root to other parts of the plant, and glucose produced through photosynthesis from the leaves to other parts of the plant.

Leaves conduct photosynthesis, through which plant food is created, as well as transpiration, in which excess water evaporates from their porous surface into the environment.

Flowers are the reproductive organs of a plant. They have many different possible forms, and normally contain an ovule, which becomes a seed. Some flowers produce fruit around their seeds as protection.

WATER AND OXYGEN

The use of hydroponics ensures a plant has ready access to a critical resource—water. Water is used by a plant to carry nutrients around its structure and as a raw material for capturing light energy and turning that energy into sugars through photosynthesis. It also serves a secondary function of evaporative cooling.

A plant's roots also need oxygen, primarily to aid in the plant's respiration, bringing in oxygen and releasing carbon dioxide. The most difficult part of designing a hydroponic system is trying to resolve these two competing needs of the plant root zone: access to water and regular exposure to oxygen. A plant can normally find a good balance between these two needs in soil because of its porous structure. Of course, as many home gardeners know, it's easy to mess up that equilibrium by over- or under-watering potted plants.

HYDROPONIC SYSTEMS

Hydroponic systems have been designed to balance a plant's need for water and oxygen. Good engineers love simplicity, so whatever the method used, the fewer moving parts and the fewer electrical and plumbing connections the better. Here are some of the most popular systems.

Flood and Drain

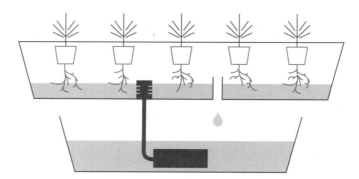

Flood and drain (aka ebb and flow) exposes roots alternately to water and air. Nutrient water is pumped up into trays and then drained down several times each day. The pumps are typically controlled by timers, allowing the system to be fully automated. The system is simple and works well, but you have to be precise in getting the water height correct.

Deep Water Culture (DWC)

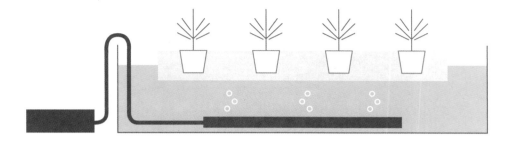

Deep water culture consists of big trays full of bubbling water. The aim is to heavily oxygenate the nutrient water in which the roots sit by creating visible or microscopic bubbles. The plants sit in holes in floating "rafts" on the water. Some call DWC, confusingly, a "shallow raft system." This is my favorite system because it's simple and doesn't cause a lot of stress on the plants if the power should go off unexpectedly.

Nutrient Film Technique (NFT)

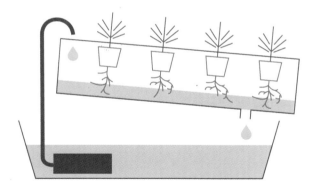

In an NFT system, water is pumped up from a reservoir and trickled down an array of channels. The plants sit in holes in the channels, with their roots exposed to air and water. Although a popular choice for greenhouses, this system does have a downside—because of the large number of channels and connections, the plumbing gets kind of complicated, to say the least.

Kratky Method

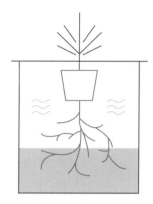

In simple terms, this is a system of growing plants in a water solution without the use of pumps, air stones, or anything else to provide oxygen to the plants' roots. The Kratky method suspends a plant's roots within a growing medium just at the top of a water reservoir. As the roots absorb the water, the level of the water drops and the roots grow, creating an air gap where the roots are exposed to oxygen. This approach is probably the easiest way to try hydroponics at home, but it can also be used in larger-scale situations in which electricity is not available.

Dutch Bucket

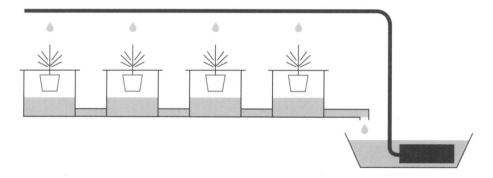

Dutch bucket (aka bato bucket) is a system with a main reservoir and a single watering line entering buckets filled with a hydroponic growing medium. Each bucket also has a drain line that is connected to a main drain. This system is great for larger plants and is very simple for home growers to use outdoors or indoors. You can start small, with just one or two buckets, but this approach can also be scaled up to massive sizes. Many commercial hydroponic cucumber and tomato growers use Dutch buckets in arrays of hundreds or even thousands of units. The main advantage is flexibility, as you can easily have different-size buckets growing different types of plants.

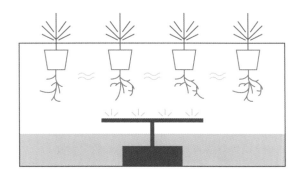

These are systems that aerosolize a nutrient solution into superfine droplets and then either spray (aeroponics) or "fog" (fogponics) that solution around the roots of plants. In both cases, the nutrient solution is normally applied at timed intervals, rather than continuously, to ensure the roots have enough access to oxygen. These methods can stimulate very fast growth but are not always easy to manage and maintain. Fogponics has become popular in cannabis cultivation because, if done well, it can foster massive root structures and thus very large plants. In states where commercial cannabis growers are restricted on the number of plants they can grow, this allows them to maximize yield by growing immense plants.

ROOT SUPPORT

A seemingly simple question is whether a plant will grow without the physical support of soil. The answer is actually quite complex. In hydroponics, two common approaches are used to support a plant.

Soil-Like Support

In this method, you use a growing medium that mimics the structure of soil, which means a porous substance that roots can push through and that also suspends some moisture and allows for air pockets. It can be used for the entirety of the root system, or for just part of the root system, with other parts dangling freely.

Here are some of the most common soil-like growing mediums used today:

1. Rockwool, a spun stone–chalk substrate
2. Coconut husk (aka coco husk), either loose or packed into "plugs," often mixed with perlite volcanic pellets
3. Recycled carpet (especially for microgreens)
4. Combinations of biopolymers and natural fibers, such as BioStrate
5. Rooting sponges, made of coconut husk and peat

1

Minimal Support

In this approach, you support the "neck" of the plant only, allowing its roots to dangle freely, as long as their water and oxygen requirements are fulfilled.

In a hydroponic system, young plants and cuttings are often placed in simple collars that provide this kind of minimal support but allow roots to develop. As the plant grows, additional support structure or growing medium can be placed around the shoulder between the root and the stem. This is primarily for physical support, however, and not always necessary for nutrient absorption.

As was proved by a 2010 experiment on the International Space Station, root systems can grow with or without gravity. So while we associate root growth with plant support, as long as there is something physical holding the stem of a plant upright, it can and will happily continue growing. With a bigger, healthier root system, the plant will absorb more nutrients and become large and strong. For creeping varieties like lemon balm and thyme, plants will happily grow along a flat surface with very little support from any root structure.

Inventors have recently patented minimal support systems called mesh substrates, in which plants are seeded in mesh sheets or expandable netting. These have the advantage of being reusable and of allowing growers to plant seeds very tightly together. As the plants grow, the netting can be gradually expanded to allow space for the plants' larger size without crowding.

PLANT NUTRITION

When planting in soil, growers often take plant nutrition for granted and forget about the individual nutrients a plant needs. They add general "fertilizer" to encourage plant growth without thinking too much about what is in the fertilizer. In hydroponics, we are ensuring that the nutrients required by the plant are all there in sufficient quantities for the plant to thrive. That means the nutrient solution has to be "complete" for us to have success.

The Hoagland Solution

Thankfully, plant nutrition is far simpler than human nutrition. One of the great strides in hydroponics was the development of the Hoagland solution in the late 1930s. This was an attempt to describe all the mineral macro- and micronutrients a plant needs. The solution looks complex but is really just a "recipe" for combining minerals in the right ratios for a plant to grow. Each component is expressed in parts per million (ppm). You do not need to know or remember the exact quantities, but it's good to know what feeds your plant.

Today, most commercially available nutrient solutions are still based on the Hoagland formula, with some tweaks.

Element	Parts Per Million (ppm)
Potassium (K)	235
Nitrogen (N)	210
Calcium (Ca)	200
Sulfur (S)	64
Magnesium (Mg)	48
Phosphorus (P)	31
Iron (Fe)	1 to 5
Boron (B)	0.5
Manganese (Mn)	0.5
Zinc (Zn)	0.05
Copper (Cu)	0.02
Molybdenum (Mo)	0.01

For home growers, there is little need to worry about the precise nutrient formula you are buying, unless you start to focus on growing more and more of a very specific type of plant. Nutrient solutions are added to the water in a hydroponic system, either by mixing a powder into a water container and then pouring the mixture into the hydroponic reservoir, or by buying a nutrient mix already in liquid form. Liquid nutrients are more expensive, but they are much easier to work with for a new grower. When dosing small home hydroponic systems, the level of nutrients you need to add is very small (but we'll get to that later).

Nutrient Balance

Hydroponic nutrient solutions are made of minerals and salts. Tap water, especially if further purified or distilled, has very low levels of these dissolved solids, and as we saw earlier with John Woodward's experiments on mint in different types of water (see page 18), river water has higher levels of them.

The more minerals and salts there are in a liquid, the easier it is for electricity to pass through it—that is, it becomes more electrically conductive. So the more nutrient solution you put into plain water, the more electrically conductive it becomes. This is why serious growers measure the electrical conductivity (EC) of a water solution, which tells them if they have the right level of nutrient solution in the water. If the EC is too low, they will add more nutrients. If the EC is too high, more water is added. It might seem like a good idea just to throw in lots of nutrients, but plants will react badly to this oversupply. They can absorb far too much of specific elements into their structure, resulting in burned leaf tips or even completely disfigured leaves. So it's good to try to stick to a very specific EC level. The EC may change over time, as water evaporates and plants absorb nutrients. In systems where the water level is designed to stay constant, nutrients normally need to be added along with new water to keep the EC at the right level.

In a Kratky system (see page 28), however, it's ideal for the water to evaporate at roughly the same speed as a plant absorbs nutrients, meaning that the concentration of nutrients stays the same. Because of this nice little trick, for some plants, like a head of lettuce that is completely harvested, you can often insert nutrients at the beginning and then avoid needing to adjust the nutrient balance for its remaining six- to eight-week life cycle. Pretty cool.

Hydroponic nutrient solutions are carefully balanced so that plants get sufficient quantities of each and every mineral. As mentioned above, some plants are hungrier for certain nutrients over others, such as iron versus magnesium, so if you're trying to be perfect, you'll find a nutrient mix that is optimized more for what you are growing. But most of the time, especially at home, a general one-size-fits-all approach with an off-the-shelf nutrient solution is absolutely fine.

pH

When you add nutrients, the pH (the measure of acidity or alkalinity) of your nutrient solution will change because of the presence of minerals and salts. Growers can add so-called liquid buffers to move that pH up or down a little to target the right level of acidity. Common culinary plants are generally looking for a pH of around 6.0, given the balance of nutrients that these plants respond to.

People talk about plants liking acidic or alkaline soil. The main reason is that specific plants are "hungrier" for certain nutrients over others, and the pH at which different minerals and salts are more readily absorbed varies. For example, a plant that is iron-hungry will prefer an acidic soil because iron is easier to absorb at a lower pH. Why? That's beyond the scope of this book, but if you really want to know, get out your old chemistry textbook.

Algae

A side effect of adding nutrients to water for your plants is that you're creating a great environment for other things to grow, too—especially algae. After algae spores are blown into the room where a hydroponic system sits, they will thrive in the warm, nutrient-rich environment where the energy, carbon dioxide, and water they need are available. In small quantities, algae are not a huge problem. But they compete for the same nutrients as your plants, and when they die, microscopic fungi and fungus gnats can also be attracted to the area. So it's best to keep algae growth to a minimum.

When you look at most hydroponic systems, you'll notice that the majority of the water is hidden from view. This is to reduce the amount of light falling on the water to a minimum, which is the best way to avoid the growth of algae. You may still see the little green organisms on the growing medium of young plants, but this is okay. Generally, if your plants are thriving at home, algae are nothing to worry about.

Bacteria and Beneficial Fungi

It would be wrong to suggest that soil contains nothing but the exact nutrient solution you might use in hydroponics. There are millions of other tiny organisms in soil that help create a rich ecosystem. Each year, new information is being discovered on the interactions among these organisms.

For example, some fungi live together with roots to their mutual benefit. These mycorrhizal relationships provide the fungi with a place to live, and the fungi help keep roots clean and improve the plant's water and nutrient uptake. The details of this symbiotic relationship are still being investigated, but it seems that the fungi speed up the process of nutrient breakdown. Beneficial bacteria can also play a role around the plant's root zone to push out other, less-friendly bacteria. They may assist in the uptake of specific micronutrients as well.

Experienced hydroponic growers sometimes add these beneficial organisms to their growing system, predominantly around the root zone of plants, especially the most oxygenated areas. The current consensus seems to be that these beneficial bacteria and fungi do not affect the taste or appearance of the plants and can assist with growth speed and overall health. Over the next few decades, much more will be learned about these valuable organisms, but for simple systems at home, there is no need to worry too much about them. Your plants can be healthy, happy, and taste great without resorting to complex additions to the nutrient solution.

Aquaponics and Nutrients

As mentioned earlier, aquaponics is an adaptation of hydroponics where fish excrement is used as a source of nutrients in what is designed to be a complete system. The plants (or some plant waste) may in turn nourish the fish, and the fish are eaten at the end of their lifespan. These closed-loop systems sound simple but usually turn out to require a special finesse to design and sustain, and always require an addition of other nutrients, bacteria, fungi, or food for the fish.

I'm not a huge fan of aquaponics. The freshwater fish (usually tilapia) live a pretty depressing life in a plastic bucket and have a flavor that is not always pleasant on the palate. Since hydroponic nutrients are readily available, cheap, and easy to work with, most hydroponic growers, especially commercial growers, stick to the simple approach of buying their nutrients.

LIGHT

Sunlight

Plants have evolved and adapted to thrive in the kind of light that exists in their native environments during a normal daily cycle. For example, a basil plant that originated in the Middle East expects fairly strong, consistent access to sunlight and will flower after a few months of such exposure. This means that if you were to attempt growing this plant at home, you should make sure it has consistent access to bright sunlight. On the other hand, a woodland plant like salad burnet that is used to growing in a tree-shaded environment and even thrives in snow, should be grown away from too much direct sun. You can encourage a plant to flower by moving it into more direct sunlight, and conversely, you can return it to a vegetative stage by trimming it back aggressively over multiple weeks and reducing its exposure to sunshine. Many of the herbs you might try to grow at home hydroponically do not have demanding light requirements, so you'll be able to provide the kind of light they need pretty easily.

In the Northern Hemisphere, south-facing windows get considerable heat and direct light, which can be great for succulents and some flowers. Herbs and more delicate plants typically require less light, so you will want to position them to receive more shade during a good portion of the day. Western exposure typically brings hotter light for six to eight hours and can be good for some sun-loving varieties. North-facing windows generally receive even light throughout the day, which is ideal for plants sensitive to scorching rays, like prayer plants or begonias. Eastern exposure gets great light from early morning into the early afternoon, but is shielded from the hot afternoon sun, making it a perfect environment for a variety of indoor plants.

Artificial Light

While plants have clearly evolved to thrive in sunlight, interesting research has been done over the past few decades to test what portions of the visible and invisible light spectrum are used by plants and to what effect. As you become more interested in hydroponics and growing indoors, you might start to look into different kinds of artificial light that emphasize particular colors, and even ultraviolet. For example, plants that live on the rain forest floor primarily receive light filtered through the leaves of other plants—effectively green light. Does this mean they may grow better if the green parts of the spectrum are emphasized? Should they receive less ultraviolet light as well? Or will they thrive on full-spectrum light? Scientists are looking into this as well as what kind of light is best for what part of the life cycle of the plant. Many plants flower toward the end of the summer, when the days are starting to shorten and the light is starting to have more yellow and red in the spectrum, rather than being pure white. This is part of the reason many cannabis growers use redder lights as they push their plants to flower.

Commercial growers talk about a daily light integral, which is a combination of the intensity of the light and how long the plant is exposed to it. For example, six hours of direct sun might be equivalent to twelve hours of indirect light. When growing under artificial light, most growers use between sixteen and twenty hours of light per day during a plant's "vegetative" phase and then may reduce this amount to twelve light hours and twelve dark hours for the "flowering" phase.

How much should you worry about this when you are just starting to grow plants indoors hydroponically? Not much. A windowsill with a few hours of direct sunlight during the day is normally enough.

CHAPTER TWO

Hydroponics at Home

In this chapter, I'll walk you through how to grow hydroponically at home—from where to source your seeds and how to start them, to how to care for the plant as it grows, and then harvest it when it's time. Now that you know the underlying history and science of hydroponics, I'll teach you how to replicate these principles on a smaller scale. You might have grown soil-based plants before to different levels of success, but even if you've never touched a seed, you may find that you'll triumph with hydroponics, which is less complicated than growing plants in soil.

When it comes to choosing what kinds of plants to grow, I'm a big proponent of herbs and microgreens. While you can be more ambitious and theoretically grow any kind of vegetable or fruit plant hydroponically, herbs and microgreens will grow faster and you'll get to enjoy the benefits of your efforts sooner. They are also quite easy to maintain, and you don't need very much space to get them started.

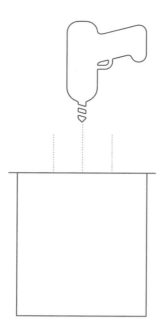

1

2

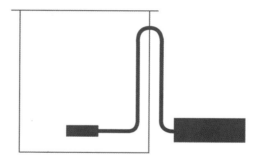

3

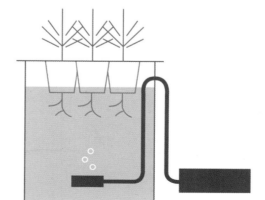

MAKING YOUR OWN
HYDROPONIC SYSTEM

You can make a simple hydroponic system at home using something as small as a glass or Mason jar. Here, I'll show you how to make a medium-size system using a large bucket and a few other parts, all available from a hardware store or online. This will be a deep water culture system of bubbling nutrient solution with plants resting on top.

Parts and Tools
- 1 black, food-safe 5-gallon plastic bucket with lid
- Power drill with $^3/_{16}$-inch and $1^3/_4$-inch drill bits
- 3 net pots, each 3 by $1^3/_4$ inches
- 1 small aquarium air pump
- 3-foot-length aquarium airline tubing
- 1 to 3 aquarium air stones (for breaking down the incoming air into tiny bubbles)
- Nutrient solution
- Seeds of choice
- Loose growing medium of choice (such as rockwool cubes, peat-based plugs, or the like)

1. Holding the plants
Have your bucket and lid handy. Using the drill fitted with the $1^3/_4$-inch bit, drill three $1^3/_4$-inch, evenly spaced holes in the bucket lid (the holes can form a triangle or a line). Drop a net pot into each hole.

2. Bubbling the air
Using the drill fitted with the $^3/_{16}$-inch bit, drill a hole near the top of the bucket for the airline. Connect one end of the airline to the air stone or stones, drop the end with the stone into the bucket, and thread the airline through the hole to the outside of the bucket. Connect the other end of the airline to the air pump.

3. Bringing it together
Fill the bucket with water up to $^1/_2$ inch above where the bottoms of the net pots will be once

the lid is in place. Dose the water with nutrient solution according to the brand's instructions. Turn on the air pump. Plant your seeds in their growing medium and place them in the net pots. Monitor the water level over the first few days to make sure the growing medium stays wet. As the plants shoot out roots, the water should stay roughly at the level of the roots. Check the nutrient dose level every few days and top up water or nutrients as required.

BUILDING SOMETHING LARGER

The hydroponics marketplace is well stocked with different parts and accessories, making it possible to build almost any kind of system you like. You can buy off-the-shelf components or make systems entirely from scratch using plumbing parts. So much is offered that deciding what to do can be a little overwhelming.

One of the best sets of standard parts is available from a company called +farm (see Resources, page 184), which uses a standard set of shelving units and different drip, NFT, and DWC setups, depending on what you want to achieve. The site provides full instructions and great specifications on what to buy. For someone who wants to go beyond a hobby, this is a great way to get started.

BUYING OFF-THE-SHELF SYSTEMS

Every year, more off-the-shelf hydroponic systems appear on the market. There are systems for growing a single plant up to complex setups costing thousands of dollars that can grow a significant amount of produce each month. Here's a quick overview of the products available now, for every budget (see Resources, page 184, for more information on these products).

Microgreen Kits
Growing cress and microgreens can be as simple as sprinkling seeds on a damp paper towel. But kits are available in stores and online that provide everything you need to grow a few trays each week. They normally include the growing medium, seeds, trays, and often humidity domes. For a sleek all-in-one solution, the HAMAMA kit uses specially made growing "mats," preseeded with the right density of microgreen seeds.

Small Systems: Kratky Vases
There are a few attractive small Kratky systems (see page 28). These can be simple like the Urban

Leaf, which is a neat plug designed to be inserted in the neck of a wine bottle, or expensive high-quality products like the Amphora from Cloud Farm, which looks like a fancy vase.

Medium Systems: Tabletop LED-Lit Units

Several tabletop hydroponic and aeroponic growing systems are now available, including AeroGarden, Click & Grow, SproutsIO, and AVA. These tend to use prepackaged pods consisting of seeds already in the growing medium, often completed with added nutrients. These systems are easy to set up and get growing and are often attractive and simple to maintain, but their lights can be underpowered and the replacement pods are often very pricey. It is possible to use these systems with growing mediums and seeds you purchase yourself, which will dramatically reduce the cost.

Large Systems: Tower Garden

The Tower Garden is a modular, self-contained aeroponic system that can be used indoors or outdoors. It consists of a reservoir at the base and a set of circular trunk sections up the middle, usually stacked around five to six feet tall. Plants are fitted into sites that stick out of the trunk. The nutrient solution flows up the middle and trickles down past the sites.

PLANTING AND GROWING

SEEDS

Generally, any seed you can grow in soil can be grown hydroponically. In other words, there's no need to look for special hydroponic seeds. When using seeds for popular herbs and plants like basil, parsley, or lettuce, your germination rates—the percentage of seeds that sprout successfully—should be close to 100 percent. This is because there is a huge market for these seeds, and they have been commercially optimized to sprout easily. With more rare and specialized plant varieties, your germination rate might be far lower. Sometimes no more than 10 percent of your seeds will germinate successfully. This is natural and is nothing to worry about, but it's important to know before you start questioning your abilities as a hydroponic grower.

Seeds come in all kinds of shapes and sizes, and commercially popular seeds might also be pelleted or primed. Pelleted seeds have been coated with a simple inert material (mainly clay) to make them all uniform. This is popular among commercial growers, as they plant thousands or millions of seeds a day, but it doesn't make much difference to home growers, so don't be concerned if the seeds you buy have not been pelleted. Primed seeds have been presoaked to kick off the very first part of the germination stage and then dried again to "freeze" that stage in time. Once they are moistened and planted, they will rapidly germinate fully—up to around 50 percent more quickly. Don't worry too much about the difference, as home growers can use seeds of any type without difficulty.

For some kinds of plants, you might need to presoak your seeds in water to soften their shell and speed germination. For others, you may wish to soak or rinse the seeds in a diluted hydrogen peroxide solution. The hydrogen peroxide can achieve two things: it removes any bacteria or potential fungi on the seed shell and it can break down the seed shell so that germination itself happens more quickly and reliably. Look at the advice from your seed provider for precise instructions.

There's no need to be too precious about the sources of your seeds. Seeds are mostly very affordable, so have fun and experiment. Some of the best crops I've grown have been from experimental purchases, often made on impulse just to see what a particular plant might taste like.

In the United States, Johnny's Selected Seeds is one of the largest seed suppliers, and it has a fantastic range of stock. The germination rates are reliable, the seeds are well packaged, and their website provides a great amount of information. Other great suppliers include Baker Creek Heirloom Seeds, Kitazawa Seed Company, and, especially for violas, Stokes Seeds. As a home grower, you can order seeds for culinary plants grown around the world, so keep searching for the most exciting plants out there. (For more recommended seed sources, see Resources, page 184.)

GROWING MEDIUMS

Many different growing mediums can be used for a home hydroponics system (see page 26 for a more complete breakdown). You can buy them at your local hydroponics garden store (see Resources, page 184)—most larger cities now have more than one—or online. They come in many different sizes, so the main choices are in the type of medium and the size of sheet or plug you want. You should choose a medium that fits inside your planting vessel.

Some growing mediums, like rockwool, need to be soaked in water before using. It helps balance the pH and washes off any dust. These mediums do not need to be soaked in a nutrient solution.

PLANTING

Planting consists simply of placing your seed (presoaked or not) into your growing medium, then spraying or dripping a little water on it so both are saturated. Your growing medium must be in a situation in which it will stay saturated. You don't want your seeds to dry out.

In a Kratky system, the water should always be at least touching either the growing medium or the plant's roots—whichever is lower. You may need to top up the water to keep it at this point, so check the level every couple of days. Do not overfill the water once the roots are growing, as they need an air gap to have access to oxygen. If you are using a growing medium, you don't need to pour water directly on it if it is touching water from below or if the plant's roots have access to water.

Until a seed has sprouted, there's no need to have any light falling on it. In fact, seeds are usually germinated in the dark. But once the seed has sprouted, you definitely want light to reach the seedling so it doesn't stretch out and lose pigmentation while desperately trying to find a light source (as it would if buried deep under soil). Depending on the variety, a very slight amount of stretching might be preferable.

STRETCHING THE SHOOT

When seeds are buried deep under the surface of the soil, or when they simply don't have a reliable source of light, they sprout shoots that are longer than regular shoots, stretching upward to find additional light the plant needs. This results in a plant that is different in shape (longer) and color (lighter) than it would normally be if it were exposed to sufficient light. You can test this on any grass lawn: place a cardboard box upside down anywhere on the lawn to deprive a small area of sunlight. In a few days, you'll see the stretching and a pale color where the grass was covered.

These variations in shape and color are desirable with certain plants, and the plant's appearance is purposefully altered by keeping it in the dark when germinating. A good example of this is *kaiware*, an Asian microgreen for which a lighter-colored stem is often desirable, so it's kept

in the dark longer to develop this way. Another example is "forced rhubarb," which is grown under clay pots or in sheds to achieve stalks that are green-yellow, very long, and softer than regular red rhubarb.

HUMIDITY AND SPROUTING

Seeds generally sprout faster in a humid environment, which can be achieved by placing a transparent dome over your germinating seeds. But once a seed has sprouted and has a little growth, too much humidity will encourage mold and may inhibit the plant's basic functions, like photosynthesis, transpiration, and respiration. At that point, it's important to remove any cover. However, as long as the growing medium is saturated with water or nutrient solution, it's okay to go without a dome if you like. It's definitely not essential.

After a few days, you should get to the stage at which a seed has just sprouted its first cotyledons—those teensy first sprouts, normally two but occasionally just one or sometimes more than two. Plants with two cotyledons are called "dicots." Inside these sprouts is a food reserve for the plant, to be used until the plant can extract enough energy and nutrition from the sun and the soil (that is, begin photosynthesis). After that stage, the cotyledons either start photosynthesizing or drop away. In some types of plant, they last for only a few days; within others, they can exist for a year or more.

HARVESTING

Harvest time is when you finally get to reap the benefits of your hydroponic growing and tear off some stems, leaves, flowers, or even buds of your new plants for consumption (depending on the variety). The right time to harvest is dependent on the size of your plants. If you start too early, the plant will never have a chance to reach its full size that will enable it to recover quickly after harvesting. Most plants are ready to harvest four to six weeks after planting, which should give them enough recovery power to grow back the parts you've cut.

Harvesting techniques differ slightly for different kinds of plants: ones with branches, ones that are stalks, and ones that are hedges. Here is a breakdown of each type, plus directions for reaping flowers and microgreens.

BRANCHES

We call these "branching" plants because their structure is very recognizable—a little like how a child might draw a plant. A central stem splits into two, and from that split, two additional branches might sprout. These plants can be very productive if you harvest them correctly, as you are helping them produce more branches and thus more leaves. Basil, shiso, and certain varieties of mint are all branching plants.

To harvest, cut just above the node. This facilitates new growth, as the node contains more rooting hormone to encourage branching. If you harvest correctly, your plant will become bushier, with more nodes creating more leaves on the plant. Generally, you should also remove (and eat) any buds and flowers, unless, for example, you really want to grow basil flowers in abundance. Depending on the variety, once the plant starts flowering, the leaves will often change in flavor and appearance, normally to their detriment. Don't be shy. When a plant is established and growing fast, it's better to cut it back more and reap the benefits than to be too cautious. If the plant is flourishing, you should be able to cut from it every week or so for home use. Feel free to prune any leaves that are dying or discolored because of lack of light.

STALKS

Other plants—such as parsley and cilantro—don't have a branching structure. Instead, they shoot out multiple stalks from a single base. Sometimes people are confused about how to harvest these plants, as they assume the stalks will grow back (they won't). If you just cut the leaves from the stem, the stem itself will dry out and shrivel up and you'll only have to remove it later. Instead, cut the whole stem from its base. Parsley and similar plants will keep sprouting brand new stems for a long time if kept in good growing conditions. Also, don't discard the stems. For example, parsley stems have a sharper flavor and are less delicate than the leaves, so they work well in long-cooked stocks, stews, and braises, rather than in "fresh" dishes. They can be finely chopped, tied with kitchen twine in a little bundle with other aromatic herbs for a *bouquet garni*, or enclosed with other herbs in a cheesecloth bundle called a *sachet d'épices*.

HEDGES

For plants that creep and grow with many strands—such as thyme, oregano, marjoram, and some mints—the job of harvesting is easy. Simply cut back a handful of strands a few inches at a time. These will regrow and other stems will pop back to join them. Some of these varieties are slow growing, so it may take at least a couple of weeks until you can harvest again.

FLOWERS

Harvesting flowers is quick and easy. As you would expect, trim the stem. There is no purpose in leaving a length of stem, so feel free to cut it right back to the node.

Harvesting microgreens is simple. Lift the "mat" of microgreens and their growing medium out of its tray. While grabbing a bunch from the top, use scissors to cut horizontally across the stems so that you can pull the bunch free. Be careful to keep your fingers away from the blade.

HOW TO TAKE CUTTINGS

A "cutting" is a section of the plant that can be used for propagation—that is, to start a whole new plant. It basically means you cut off a piece of a source plant and then plant it in a growing medium, which can be soil or a hydroponic nutrient solution. If you do it correctly, a new plant should start forming from the cutting within a few weeks.

There are two great reasons to take cuttings. First, you get to enjoy plants that cannot be grown from seed, such as some unusual varieties of mint or basil. Second, you can get to a full-size plant much faster—often twice as fast—than growing from seed.

If you're worried about damaging your original plant by cutting it, fear not. You're doing the same amount of cutting as you would while harvesting, and if you choose a mature adult plant, it should be able to recover rather quickly. Here is how to do it:

1. Choose a source plant that is at least six to eight inches tall. It needs to be mature enough that you can take a cutting without decimating the original plant.
2. Select a healthy branch or part of the main stem that is three to five inches long.
3. Cut just above the branching node. This area often has more rooting hormones within it, making it easier for your cutting to grow roots. Cut cleanly. Never tear or crush the stem.
4. Remove leaves from the bottom of the shoot, leaving about four inches of clean stem. Rooting hormones are available that you can dip the stem into to improve the chance of success, but they are not normally needed.
5. Insert the stem into a foam collar (see page 32) or deep into growth medium in your hydroponic system. After around a week, you should start to see small root hairs growing at the bottom of the stem, a sign that the cutting is beginning to thrive.

Many plants grow especially well from cuttings. Mint is a voracious grower, and basil is a good candidate, too. Some hardier, slower-growing plants, like rosemary and sage, are more difficult. But there's very little risk, so why not give it a try with the next cool plant you see?

Using cuttings will give you a head start, without having to wait through a plant's early stages, and it's also a great way to share different rare plants among friends. If you're feeling adventurous, you can even grab cuttings from wild plants. Make sure you are not taking from a private or protected area, and ensure no pests are on the plants. You can eliminate most pests by wiping the leaves and stem down with a little diluted rubbing alcohol.

You may even choose to take a large number of cuttings from the same plant to replicate its characteristics in several plants. These clones are genetically identical to the original, so they should display the same visual appearance and taste when grown under the same conditions.

DEALING WITH PESTS

The key reason many people choose to seek out an "organic" label is because they are looking for foods free of pesticides. In fact, organic certification allows some pesticide usage, for example spraying with spinosad and pyrethrum, both of which are natural insecticides. This is not to judge the safety of organic produce, but rather to say that it's hard to find produce that hasn't had some kind of pest treatment.

At home, because you are normally growing far fewer plants, pests may not be a problem if your space is clean and well ventilated. But you might encounter pests like aphids, thrips, spider mites, and others. Generally, the solution is to be attentive and use three complementary approaches. By acting quickly, most pest problems won't get out of hand.

1. Wash or wipe off the leaves with water to dislodge any insects you find.
2. Apply a little neem oil in the evening (do not use it in strong light). This oil comes from the neem tree and repels many insects and fungi. The plant can also, to a certain extent, absorb the oil for longer-term protection. Neem oil, which you'll find at most garden supply stores, is safe to use on culinary plants, but follow the directions carefully to avoid overuse (which could damage the plants).
3. Introduce beneficial insects like ladybugs and lacewings if you have sufficient plants to justify bringing them in.

CHAPTER THREE

What to Grow and How to Use It

This chapter will teach you how to grow individual plants and offer some tips on cooking with them and pairing them with other flavors in your kitchen. So you might wonder—where do the herb flavors and aromas come from?

When tasting a wine, we focus intensely on its aromas and flavor, using careful vocabulary to describe our sensory experience. This same complexity is present in edible plants and herbs, and it requires careful attention and time to discern. This is a world where the deeper we go, the richer the experience. A tour around an herb farm or a trip to a farmers' market can be a sensory journey just as exciting as a wine or beer tasting. A home full of culinary plants can be a small window into this world.

The smells you get from fresh herbs mainly come from what are called "volatile flavor compounds" or "volatiles." These are oils and other compounds in the plant. The oils can also kill microbes and fungi that might try to infect the plant. Many of these are terpenes, a large and diverse class of organic compounds that is produced by plants but also by some insects. This insect association is significant: one of the purposes of volatiles in herbs and other plants is to act as a repellent, telling insects, snails, and animals "don't eat me." Some plants can modify these fragrances to signal other plants nearby, or even parts of the same plant, that an attack is in progress, stimulating nearby cells and plants to create a chemical defense.

Anecdotally, this seems to be true when we cut a little pápalo on the farm. The aroma it gives off is very fragrant. Pápalo contains sabinene, a terpene that's also found in the holm oak and Norway spruce; myrcene, found in bay, cannabis, thyme, parsley, cardamom, and hops; and a high level of limonene, which in its most common form gives off a smell of oranges. Even when we cut just a little pápalo for a sample, the smell travels rapidly around the room, creating what seems to be a far stronger effect than should be attributed to only a few stems. Fortunately, I love it.

Coming back to more common herbs, we find that each variety of basil has many different volatiles, but they all have four main volatiles that vary considerably in their intensity: methyl chavicol (estragole, found in tarragon, fennel, and anise), linalool (which has coriander, floral, lemon, and rose notes), methyl eugenol (which has a clove-like aroma), and methyl cinnamate (found in the highest intensities in eucalyptus but also in fruits like strawberries). Some basils have far more of an anise note, for example, probably due to increased levels of methyl chavicol and trans-anethole (another compound) in these particular varieties. The flavor of spearmint, in contrast, comes from menthol and from carvone, which is found abundantly in oils from caraway seeds, as well as from dill and citrus peel.

Once you start to discover some of these components and what foods they are common in, you can see how some flavor pairings are made—though not always! Sometimes the same flavor compounds in two different ingredients can create an unappetizing pairing, which you might find out only with some kitchen experimentation.

ACTIVATING FLAVORS AND AROMAS IN YOUR HERBS

When you walk around an herb garden or put your nose up to a plant, what you are smelling is a very low-level release of aroma, probably released by air gently agitating the plants. When you place an herb leaf on your tongue, you normally won't taste anything. It's mostly by crushing and chewing that you produce flavor and aroma. Because of this, if you pop an herb straight into your mouth and chew, most of the taste you experience is via retronasal olfaction, which is a fancy way of saying that you smell it through the opening to your nose at the back of your mouth. The only downside of this is that you may find it hard to separate the dual sensations of the taste of the herb with the aromas generated upon chewing.

I often invite people touring the Farm.One to "spank" (that is, smack them between the palms of their hands) or tear certain herbs and smell deeply before eating them. Bartenders will do the same thing to an herb before using it in a drink. Spanking a mint or a hairy basil leaf activates the flavor compounds found on its exterior, which tend to have less of a grassy, vegetal character (found in almost all herbs and greens) and more of the herb-specific volatiles that characterize that particular plant. You can also just rub the underside of two leaves together, which tends to bring out citrusy, herbal, and floral notes without the grassiness.

If you're pulling herbs from a newly opened container, their characteristic smell should jump out at you instantly. As you lift out the stalks and leaves, they should give off more and more aroma as they brush against one another. If they don't, the plant is old and tired and is likely past its prime.

PRESERVING YOUR PLANTS

The herbs and plants that take the longest to grow tend to survive the best during long cooking. Rosemary, sage, thyme, and oregano (as well as oregano's relatives, marjoram and nepitella) do well in slow-cooked stews, roasts, and sauces. The same is usually true of herbs you dry, a process that oxidizes and removes some of the volatile compounds and intensifies the flavor.

Normally, I prefer cooking with fresh herbs, even when using aromatics like rosemary, because the experience of handling the fresh herb is more pleasurable and the herb can be used at the start of the dish to create a flavor base and then in moderation closer to the end to add freshness. But sometimes preserving herbs for later is useful, usually because you have an over abundance in your garden that you want to keep for a long period of time.

Your main options for preservation are air-drying; drying in an oven, dehydrator, or microwave; or freezing. Drying the herbs will intensify their flavor and remove some of the fresher aroma notes. Freezing and thawing will give you something more similar to the fresh taste.

AIR-DRYING

If you live in a relatively dry climate, air-drying herbs is easy. Aromatic herbs like rosemary, sage, and oregano do well with this method. Simply tie a small bunch of stems together with string and place them in a paper bag. Poke a few holes in the bag and then hang it upside down in a dry area of your home. This method will take around a week.

DRYING IN AN OVEN OR DEHYDRATOR

Evenly spread a thin layer of whole herbs across a baking sheet. Try to make sure the stems and leaves do not overlap, as any overlapping spots will dry more slowly. Set the oven at 150°F to 175°F, place the baking sheet in the oven, and let the herbs dry for 1 to 4 hours. (You can leave the oven door cracked open to encourage airflow, depending on your oven model.) For a dehydrator, use a similar temperature but keep the door closed. The first time you use this method, check the progress after 45 minutes to see how things are going.

DRYING IN A MICROWAVE

Surprisingly, the microwave is a great tool for drying herbs while maintaining more of the color and flavor than you would in an oven or dehydrator. Lay the herbs in a sparse layer on a microwave-safe dinner plate. You can use a layer of paper towel, but make sure the towel is microwave-safe. In a standard 1000-watt microwave, try around 60 seconds for woodier aromatic herbs like sage, rosemary, oregano, and marjoram. For lighter herbs like thyme, cilantro, basil, or anise hyssop, try 30 to 45 seconds. If you have fewer herbs or a more powerful microwave, reduce the cooking time. The first time you try this, use 15-second increments to dial in the correct time for your microwave.

AFTER DRYING

Your herbs are thoroughly dried when the leaves crumble easily and fall off the stem. At this point, transfer the herbs to a canning jar or similar airtight container for long-term storage. You can use a mortar and pestle or a spice grinder to grind them first if you like, but they'll keep a little better if stored whole.

FREEZING

Whenever a living thing is frozen and thawed, the ice crystals that form and then melt break down the cell structure of the item, damaging the cell walls. The aim in freezing herbs is not only to preserve flavor but also to maintain the texture as much as possible by reducing this cell-wall damage. No solution is perfect, but usually the best method is to chop up your herbs, cover them with a light cooking oil (such as canola or an olive oil that is not too peppery), and put them in a resealable plastic bag. You can then spread the bag flat for freezing (yes, the oil will freeze). When you want to use the herb, just snap off a frozen portion and reseal the bag. Frozen herbs will keep for about 3 months, and are best used in sauces, soups, and stocks.

COOKING WITH FRESH HERBS

This is how most of us begin cooking "properly": choose a recipe that is achievable. Buy a jar of an expensive spice just so you can add a teaspoon of it to the recipe. Carefully select a wine to match the menu. Spend more money on ingredients to create a meal for two from scratch than you would if you ate at a restaurant. The herbs you are told to use come in a tiny plastic clamshell from a chilled counter in the grocery store. You have no idea where they came from. The whole thing takes three hours longer than expected.

But with more cooking experience comes more confidence. And when you have an herb garden at arm's reach, you have more freedom to experiment, to make mistakes, and to discover different flavors. Using new fresh botanical ingredients in your food becomes a kind of culinary journey of its own that will take you far beyond the simple step of buying a clamshell of basil from the supermarket. Now is the time to accelerate your culinary journey by cooking more meals, especially ones that incorporate new recipes and ingredients.

By having a mini garden of some of the most popular herbs at home, you start to pay attention to how the plants grow and how to look after them as you harvest. But most important, you get used to the absolute freshness of herbs cut just minutes before they are eaten. Compared to produce that is shipped thousands of miles, herbs cut from your garden are brighter, more aromatic, have better color, and have almost certainly better nutrition. This encourages you to use them in abundance, and your dishes are better for it.

With a broad enough selection of herbs and a visit to a farmers' market or a CSA delivery, you can use whatever you have on hand as the basis of a recipe search. The Internet has made this astoundingly easy—as simple as typing in a few ingredients and seeing what comes up. The pleasure in this stage is in a continually changing landscape of different foods, as each week the local selection will change.

There's no need to expect to be perfect from the first try. Use the resources around you. I strongly recommend a copy of *The Flavor Bible* or *The Vegetarian Flavor Bible*, both by Karen Page and Andrew Dornenburg, to uncover all kinds of unusual and exciting flavor pairings.

Looking at fennel, for example, it pairs well with mushrooms and sage. For a hearty but summery dish, you could gently sauté onions, garlic, and mushrooms fresh from the farmers' market, thinly slice some bulb fennel into the pan, chop sage leaves and stir them in until softened, and then sprinkle some bronze fennel fronds or fennel flowers on top just before serving.

Or you could move the dish in a more Asian direction by substituting star anise and grated lemongrass for the sage. Working with flavor pairings, and using the connections between ingredients, you can build dishes that are greater than the sum of their parts. It's hard to do this if your supply of fresh herbs is so limited that you feel you must be precious with every dish, which is why growing at home is so much fun and so rewarding.

PLANT PROFILES

You've come to my favorite section of the book. Here, I've handpicked a selection of some of the most exciting, flavorful, and visually compelling plants, all of which can be easily grown by a first-time hydroponic grower. Once you've succeeded in growing a couple of everyday plants like flat-leaf parsley and basil, you'll want to experiment with others that are harder to source and whose flavors you aren't as familiar with.

I've arranged the profiles into six sections. The first one includes your basic favorites, plants that are relatively familiar and that most of us are already using in a variety of ways in the kitchen. When you're whipping up a quick dinner, it can be a huge help to have some common ingredients on hand, fresh for the picking in your own kitchen. Next, I'll familiarize you with more regionally specific plants from Europe and Asia, useful categories for exploring the vast and diverse cuisines of those continents. Some of these plants may be less familiar to you, but my suggestions on how to use them in the kitchen and how to pair them with other flavors will hopefully encourage you to try some of them in your own dishes.

Next come the exotic plants, those that are probably unfamiliar to everyone who doesn't experiment with hard-to-source ingredients on a regular basis like a chef. You'll be surprised how easy it is to grow and utilize some of these. This section also includes plants that are really reserved for the most adventurous cooks among us, like the toothache plant, which causes sensations in your mouth that you didn't even know were possible. After the garden of exotics, I'll walk you through some of the best-tasting and most popular microgreens, most of which pack a vitamin and nutrient punch, and then I'll show you the ins and outs of experimenting with different varieties of the same plant by taking cuttings.

The information I've provided in each plant profile will serve as a quick reference guide—variety-specific information on how long it will take to reach the sprouting stage and harvest time, what kind of cutting technique to use once it does, the simplest ways to get the best flavor from it, and prompts for flavor pairings to aid your experimentation in the kitchen—as you're trying to decide which plants to cultivate.

EVERYDAY FAVORITES

When you decide to grow your own edible garden at home, the most popular culinary herbs are a great place to start. For example, in the United States, the commercial demand for parsley and basil is ten times greater than the demand for any other herb. This makes sense because these herbs are both highly adaptable and play major roles in Italian and other Mediterranean dishes that have long been popular on American tables. For the past five or six decades, Western food has been dominated by these two flavor profiles, which is why you see them in nearly every market.

Luckily, this also means that seed suppliers have concentrated on producing basil strains that are not only reliable to cultivate but also taste and look good. So if you're planting at home, you have a good chance of producing a healthy basil crop in about a month's time. Parsley, which is also easy to grow, will take just a few days longer.

On the flip side, sage and rosemary are some of the slowest herbs around to get started, and it will be several months before you have a good-size plant. But once that plant is established and is kept in good light and warmth, it will keep producing generously, gifting you abundantly throughout the year.

FLAT-LEAF PARSLEY

PETROSELINUM CRISPUM VAR. NEAPOLITANUM

Cultivated around the world, parsley is a little spicy, with hints of lemon and anise. It's versatile and complements numerous foods, bringing out not only their flavor but also the flavor of other herbs and spices, which is why it's a staple in many cuisines and chef's kitchens.

ORIGIN

Europe

SEED TO SPROUT

14 days

SEED TO FIRST HARVEST

35 days

HARVEST STYLE

Stalks (page 57)

CULINARY INSPIRATION

Parboil potatoes, slice them, then sauté them in a bit of olive oil. As they near the end of their cooking time, add handfuls of chopped parsley, a squeeze of juice from a lemon and a bit of its grated zest, and some thinly sliced garlic to the pan, along with salt and pepper. The parsley will mediate the strength of the garlic and is a classic pairing with the lemon.

FLAVOR AND INGREDIENT PAIRINGS

+ cilantro
+ garlic
+ olive oil
+ rosemary
+ tomato

FRENCH THYME

THYMUS VULGARIS

French thyme has an piney aroma and a warm pungent flavor and is a key ingredient in the traditional *herbes de Provence* blend. Also known as garden thyme or common thyme, it is an "improved" cultivated form of the wild thyme of the mountains of Spain and other European countries bordering on the Mediterranean, and of Turkey, Algeria, and Tunisia. Make sure to strip the leaves from the woody stems before using.

ORIGIN
Europe

SEED TO SPROUT
14 days

**SEED TO
FIRST HARVEST**
42 days

HARVEST STYLE
Hedges (page 58)

CULINARY INSPIRATION

Create a simple orange-thyme marmalade: roast orange slices with fresh orange juice and a dusting of sugar poured over them for about 40 minutes, then sprinkle them with fresh thyme, salt, pepper, and more sugar. Or you can combine dried and ground thyme leaves with sumac and sesame to make *za'atar*, a staple of the Middle Eastern spice cabinet.

FLAVOR AND INGREDIENT PAIRINGS

+ black peppercorn
+ broccoli
+ brussels sprout
+ cabbage
+ fennel

GENOVESE BASIL

OCIMUM BASILICUM 'GENOVESE'

One of the most popular basil cultivars, Genovese basil, which produces large leaves with a sweet flavor, is famous for its use in pesto. Cooking this basil is ideal, as it doesn't become bitter, even after long periods of heat.

ORIGIN
Europe

SEED TO SPROUT
10 days

SEED TO FIRST HARVEST
31 days

HARVEST STYLE
Branches (page 56)

CULINARY INSPIRATION

There are hundreds of great uses for this popular leaf, and some of the best are the easiest. Slow-roasted tomatoes dressed with a drizzle of olive oil and a sprinkle of crushed garlic, then topped with freshly torn basil leaves, are a delight.

FLAVOR AND INGREDIENT PAIRINGS

+   green tea
+   lemon zest
+   mango
+   raspberry
+   tomato

ROSEMARY

ROSMARINUS OFFICINALIS

A pine-like fragrance and a pungent flavor make rosemary a good addition to richer dishes. It can also be combined with legumes, potatoes, and squash, as well as sweet dishes like cakes and baked apples, where it discreetly adds complexity. When fresh, the delicate oils of the plant are still very present, giving off a pleasant stickiness to the touch.

ORIGIN

Europe

SEED TO SPROUT

21 days

SEED TO FIRST HARVEST

49 days

HARVEST STYLE

Stalks (page 57)

CULINARY INSPIRATION

Try a cocktail that brings out the magic combination of rosemary, lemon, and honey. Combine one part honey, two parts lemon juice, and four parts gin, then add ice and shake well. Strain into a martini glass whose rim has been rubbed with fresh, oily rosemary and garnish with a small sprig.

FLAVOR AND INGREDIENT PAIRINGS

+ basil
+ carrot
+ lemon zest
+ parsley
+ sage

SAGE

SALVIA OFFICINALIS

You may think your sage plant is in trouble because of its relatively slow start after planting, but once it reaches a height of three to four inches, it will start to grow rapidly. Best of all, if kept warm with plenty of sun, it will produce year-round. Sage works well with buttery or olive oil flavors and is used often with chicken, gnocchi, or pork. The leaves can also be deep-fried.

ORIGIN
Europe

SEED TO SPROUT
14 days

**SEED TO
FIRST HARVEST**
42 days

HARVEST STYLE
Branches (page 56)

CULINARY INSPIRATION

A quick sage pesto is a warm, unusual variation that pairs beautifully with slow-roasted meats or vegetables. Grind a handful of sage leaves with pine nuts, almonds, or even hazelnuts; plenty of olive oil; some garlic; and salt and pepper.

FLAVOR AND INGREDIENT PAIRINGS

+ apple
+ beans
+ capers
+ caraway
+ tomato

EUROPEAN KITCHEN GARDEN

When we started Farm.One, one of the driving forces was the idea of a "kitchen garden" in the heart of the city, growing whatever selection of herbs and flowers a cook might desire. It was to be the kind of garden a French country restaurant has on its property that allows the chef to walk a few steps down the path and come back with a handful of summer savory for trying out in a new dish. Known in French as a *potager*, a small kitchen garden of herbs and vegetables popular in France with both chefs and home cooks.

The plants in this section are what you might find in a kitchen garden in France, England, or, depending on the plant, in other parts of Europe. You've likely come across many of these in America, but you would be hard-pressed to find all of them at once at even the best farmers' markets. These European herbs are essential to good, simple, everyday cooking, and their use typically goes back centuries and in some cases much longer. Countless dishes are improved with the inclusion of these herbs.

Among my favorite plants in this category are those that contain notes of anise. Mainstream uses of anise and licorice flavors are often too strong (think of sweet licorice candies, for example). But anise in herbal form is usually far more delicate, as found in chervil, anise hyssop, and fennel flowers. These flavors work well with fruits, allowing you to use herbs outside of their more widely used savory context. Unfortunately these kinds of plants don't often end up in your local grocery store, so growing them at home is the best way to introduce yourself to them and expand your herbal horizons.

Another flavor strand that is rarely seen in city markets is sorrel. With its sour tang from oxalic acid, each sorrel variety has an interesting flavor and is visually striking—from long green leaves to round, stubby red-veined ones to small heart-shaped ones. The availability of sorrel varieties is limited because they are delicate and easily damaged, which means they cannot survive most transport. That's a good reason to grow at least one of the varieties at home and enjoy its acidic, citrusy notes in all kinds of savory and sweet dishes.

ANISE HYSSOP

AGASTACHE FOENICULUM

This is one of my favorite herbs. Although the plant belongs to the mint family, it has a tangy anise aroma and flowers that are a deep violet. Both the leaves and the flowers can be used as seasoning or as an ingredient in tea. Anise hyssop is native to North America's Great Plains and was once used as a medicinal herb to promote healing and reduce fevers.

ORIGIN

North America

SEED TO SPROUT

14 days

SEED TO FIRST HARVEST

42 days

HARVEST STYLE

Branches (page 56)

CULINARY INSPIRATION

To experience the clear taste of a young anise hyssop leaf with its best pairings, try a fresh Kir royale. Fill a glass with Prosecco, add some blackberries and a drop of lemon juice, and finish with a fresh anise hyssop leaf for garnish.

FLAVOR AND INGREDIENT PAIRINGS

+ apricot
+ blueberry
+ chocolate
+ milk
+ strawberry

AQUA LARGE LEAF WATERCRESS

NASTURTIUM OFFICINALE 'AQUA'

This large-leaved watercress has a hot, peppery flavor and succulent texture. The plant is typically eaten raw and can complement fish such as trout or salmon or simply enrich a salad with its big flavor.

ORIGIN
Europe

SEED TO SPROUT
14 days

**SEED TO
FIRST HARVEST**
35 days

HARVEST STYLE
Hedges (page 58)

CULINARY INSPIRATION

To experience the peppery flavor of the watercress balanced with summer-sweet ingredients, toss it in a salad bowl with sliced avocado, chopped almonds, sliced strawberries, a splash of balsamic vinegar, a little olive oil if needed, and torn mint of whatever kind you like, then season with salt and pepper.

FLAVOR AND INGREDIENT PAIRINGS

+   cabbage
+   horseradish
+   olive oil
+   rutabaga
+   turnip

AQUA LARGE LEAF WATERCRESS

BRONZE FENNEL

FOENICULUM VULGARE

This type of sweet fennel is grown more for its fronds rather than for the bulb. The fronds are a beautiful bronze color, sweet, and tender to bite and chew.

ORIGIN

Europe

SEED TO SPROUT

21 days

SEED TO FIRST HARVEST

30 days

HARVEST STYLE

Stalks (page 57)

CULINARY INSPIRATION

Roast halved fennel bulbs with garlic and caraway seeds at 325°F for about 1 hour, until soft and caramelized. Halfway through, stir some halved white mushrooms into the pan. To serve, douse with lemon juice, sprinkle with salt and pepper and perhaps some capers, then garnish generously with bronze fennel fronds.

FLAVOR AND INGREDIENT PAIRINGS

+ lemon zest
+ orange peel
+ passion fruit
+ sage
+ thyme

BRONZE FENNEL

CHERVIL

—————

ANTHRISCUS CEREFOLIUM

A delicate annual herb related to parsley, chervil is commonly used to season dishes with a milder flavor profile, such as fish, vegetables, and omelets. It also joins chives, parsley, and tarragon to make up *fines herbes*, a mainstay of French cuisine. Unlike more pungent, robust herbs or herb blends, *fines herbes* is added to dishes at the end of cooking, and the same rule applies to fresh chervil.

ORIGIN
Europe

SEED TO SPROUT
14 days

**SEED TO
FIRST HARVEST**
35 days

HARVEST STYLE
Stalks (page 57)

CULINARY INSPIRATION

For a summery appetizer, toss spiralized cucumber with the same quantity of cold cooked glass (aka cellophane) noodles, a generous measure of fresh lemon juice, a little very thinly sliced red onion, olive oil, and salt and pepper. Halve red or green grapes and add them to the mix. Chop a big handful of fresh chervil and stir it in at the last minute.

FLAVOR AND INGREDIENT PAIRINGS

+   artichoke
+   cinnamon
+   fennel bulb
+   mezcal
+   pastis

FENNEL CROWNS

FOENICULUM VULGARE

Fennel crowns are the bright yellow flowers that form at the top of fennel fronds. They have a sweet, strong anise flavor that is delightful.

CULINARY INSPIRATION

Marinate the softest parts of a thinly sliced fennel bulb and a chopped small red bell pepper in a good white balsamic or champagne vinegar, olive oil, and the juice from an orange for a half hour. If you like, add a small amount of thinly sliced hot red chile. Serve on bruschetta topped with fennel fronds and a generous sprinke of fennel crowns.

ORIGIN

Europe

SEED TO SPROUT

21 days

SEED TO FIRST HARVEST

91 days

HARVEST STYLE

Flowers (page 58)

FLAVOR AND INGREDIENT PAIRINGS

+ cilantro
+ cucumber
+ mint
+ parsley
+ potato

GREEN SORREL

RUMEX ACETOSA

The bright green leaves and stems of this plant (also known simply as sorrel) come in three sizes: micro, baby, and large. They have a tangy, sour taste that can be used to lift a savory dish like shellfish or chicken, or add character to a fresh salad. Used sparingly, they can also provide a citrusy note in a dessert like panna cotta.

ORIGIN

Europe

SEED TO SPROUT

10 days

SEED TO FIRST HARVEST

31 days

HARVEST STYLE

Stalks (page 57)

CULINARY INSPIRATION

Don't cook sorrel down too much, or its flavor and color will be lost. An asparagus or spring pea risotto is given a welcome hint of freshness with a handful of sorrel leaves stirred in just before serving. They can also be blanched, blended, and added to the risotto toward the end of cooking to color it a light green. Another option is to chop the leaves, mix them with herbs like parsley and mint, and toss with boiled potatoes, white beans, or chickpeas.

FLAVOR AND INGREDIENT PAIRINGS

+ cream
+ egg
+ fish
+ ricotta
+ spinach

LEMON BALM

MELISSA OFFICINALIS

An herb with a citrusy aroma and a hint of mint, lemon balm grows and spreads rapidly, cascading downward if left untrimmed. It is best used when fresh and raw, as its delicate flavors can be lost when cooked or dried.

ORIGIN

Europe

SEED TO SPROUT

14 days

**SEED TO
FIRST HARVEST**

35 days

HARVEST STYLE

Branches (page 56)

CULINARY INSPIRATION

A simple way to use lemon balm is to steep a big handful in a teapot of hot water for 20 minutes or so, strain, and then sweeten the infusion with honey. If you're feeling more adventurous, try a standard pesto recipe, swapping the basil for lemon balm.

FLAVOR AND INGREDIENT PAIRINGS

+   black tea
+   guava
+   lychee
+   orange
+   peach

LEMON BEEBALM

MONARDA CITRIODORA

This is a vibrant fuchsia-colored wildflower with fragrant leaves that are usable just a few weeks after planting. Also known as lemon mint or purple horsemint, lemon beebalm is part of the large mint clan, and both the colorful flowers and lemony leaves are edible. It makes for a great addition to salads and desserts.

ORIGIN

Europe

SEED TO SPROUT

14 days

SEED TO FIRST HARVEST

35 days

HARVEST STYLE

Branches (page 56)

CULINARY INSPIRATION

Use lemon beebalm sparingly in the same way you might use lemon zest, such as sprinkled on roasted mushrooms. You can also make a tea, steeping the fresh leaves in hot water for 5 to 10 minutes.

FLAVOR AND INGREDIENT PAIRINGS

+   black tea
+   damask rose
+   mint
+   raspberry
+   tomato

RED PURSLANE

PORTULACA OLERACEA SUBSP. SATIVA

Although similar in flavor to green and golden varieties, red purslane, with its reddish-green stems and large, succulent, tender leaves, has a more unusual appearance. It is frequently used in salads or as a striking visual addition to a minimal plate. Enjoy it raw to make the most of it as an ingredient.

ORIGIN

Europe

SEED TO SPROUT

14 days

SEED TO FIRST HARVEST

35 days

HARVEST STYLE

Stalks (page 57)

CULINARY INSPIRATION

Add to a potato salad along with parsley and mint. The most satisfying potato salads have far more vinegar, salt, spice, and sweetness than you'd expect. After the potatoes are done, immediately toss them with vinegar, then follow your favorite potato salad recipe. Make sure to toss the purslane in last, to give the salad crunch and freshness.

FLAVOR AND INGREDIENT PAIRINGS

+ chervil
+ cucumber
+ garlic
+ green bean
+ olive oil

RED-VEINED SORREL

RUMEX SANGUINEUS

Red-veined sorrel, also known as bloody dock or red dock, has a bold red stem and veins that run up its structured leaves, making them some of the most popular and visually striking leaves around. The flavor is sour and can be powerful depending on leaf size. Used sparingly, it can be a flavor-balancing addition to a dish.

ORIGIN

The Mediterranean

SEED TO SPROUT

21 days

SEED TO FIRST HARVEST

21 days

HARVEST STYLE

Stalks (page 57)

CULINARY INSPIRATION

These delicate, showy leaves are best used in small dishes, where their visual impact and sour flavor are given a platform to shine. Try crostini or bruschette topped with a rich pea pesto (swap out basil for peas), with a cherry tomato half and a red-veined sorrel leaf placed last for a hint of acidity.

FLAVOR AND INGREDIENT PAIRINGS

+ chive
+ green bean
+ oregano
+ parsley
+ squash

SALAD BURNET

SANGUISORBA MINOR

Salad burnet has a surprising cucumber-like aroma and flavor. Its small, round leaves with spike-shaped edges are very fine and soft, especially when grown indoors. Strip the leaves off the stems and thinly slice or roughly chop them, then toss them into a salad for a fresh, summery taste that can replace cucumber altogether.

ORIGIN

Europe

SEED TO SPROUT

10 days

SEED TO FIRST HARVEST

31 days

HARVEST STYLE

Stalks (page 57)

CULINARY INSPIRATION

Use the mild astringency of salad burnet and its delicate cucumber flavor in simple dishes. Slice silken tofu into cubes, add a squeeze of lemon and lime and a little soy sauce, and stir gently. Add finely chopped scallions and crushed peanuts. Finish this cooling starter with thinly sliced mint and salad burnet sprinkled on top.

FLAVOR AND INGREDIENT PAIRINGS

+   avocado
+   rosemary
+   tarragon
+   vinegar
+   zucchini

SALAD BURNET

VIOLA FLOWERS

VIOLA SPP.

Some members of the *Viola* genus (violets, violas, and pansies) are among the most popular edible flowers in the United States. Fresh flowers are most often used for garnishing and candying. The pungent perfume of some varieties adds sweetness, while the mild pea flavor of most other varieties combines well with both sweet and savory foods. The simple addition of a few brilliant blooms transforms any dish into an elegant presentation.

ORIGIN

Europe

SEED TO SPROUT

14 days

SEED TO FIRST HARVEST

42 days

HARVEST STYLE

Flowers (page 58)

CULINARY INSPIRATION

If these flowers have a flavor at all, it's a little like a mild pea tendril, so they're usually used for visual impact. A tip: use odd numbers of visually striking elements on a plate to create an aesthetically pleasing composition. Five flowers are usually more than enough.

FLAVOR AND INGREDIENT PAIRINGS

+ cream

+ meringue

+ mint

+ pastry

+ peas

WOOD SORREL

OXALIS VALDIVIENSIS

This plant grows small, heart-shaped leaves, often in groups of three. A member of the *Oxalis* genus (along with all other sorrel varieties), wood sorrel is high in oxalic acid, which produces a tangy, sour, and refreshing taste. The leaves should be used fresh, and they work well as an addition to salad mixes. Wood sorrel also pairs well with gamy meats and fish.

ORIGIN
North America

SEED TO SPROUT
10 days

SEED TO FIRST HARVEST
31 days

HARVEST STYLE
Stalks (page 57)

CULINARY INSPIRATION

Use the sour punch of wood sorrel leaves and flowers to sharpen this easy, sweet dessert. Soak pine nuts in white wine, stuff dates with the softened nuts, drizzle the dates with honey and dust with a pinch of nutmeg, then roast at 400°F for 15 to 25 minutes. Plate directly from the oven, add a little sea salt, and scatter wood sorrel leaves and flowers generously over the top.

FLAVOR AND INGREDIENT PAIRINGS

+   asparagus
+   nuts
+   potato
+   spinach
+   wild greens

ASIAN KITCHEN GARDEN

While living in Japan for eight years, I was constantly blown away by the quality of the local produce and by the completely different flavor palate available in the grocery stores. Having had the opportunity to travel to Vietnam, Hong Kong, China, Taiwan, Korea, and Thailand to visit farmers' markets, I was able to try ingredients that were completely new to me.

Walking through a wet market in Asia is an experience every food lover must try. There you'll come across piles of vibrant green vegetables and herbs and stocks of live animals, fish, and crustaceans, all of them exchanging hands between excited customers and poker-faced shopkeepers. Many of the items you'll see are something you probably won't recognize, let alone know how to cook. Experiencing that reemphasizes that we may have "Chinese" food in this country, but we are unfamiliar with most of Asia's ingredients.

This section contains some of the best Asian herbs I've come across, things like *rau ram* or brightly flavored green shiso—my personal favorite. Growing these herbs at home will give you a small window into the riches of Asian produce and hopefully inspire you to seek out more adventurous recipes and to shop in your local Asian grocery stores or Asian neighborhood. You'll find that it's worth hunting around where you live for produce, rather than relying on the big-name market chains that are beholden to industrial-scale delivery systems and mass-market demand.

GREEN SHISO

PERILLA FRUTESCENS VAR. CRISPA

Green shiso, also known as shiso (from Japanese) and as perilla mint, boasts beautiful, bright green leaves and stems. The plant is part of the mint family, but with a more complex and unusual flavor than many of its kin, including roasted and nutty notes with a hint of toast. Most commonly used as a garnish, battered and fried for tempura, or wrapped around sushi, in larger quantities, shiso can also be sautéed as you might spinach or other greens for a creative side dish.

ORIGIN
Asia

SEED TO SPROUT
10 days

**SEED TO
FIRST HARVEST**
31 days

HARVEST STYLE
Branches (page 56)

CULINARY INSPIRATION

Make a quick pickle of julienned daikon radish, thinly sliced wakame, ginger, and sesame seeds. After a couple of hours in the refrigerator, toss with chopped green shiso leaves and serve.

FLAVOR AND INGREDIENT PAIRINGS

+ eggplant
+ grapefruit
+ green tea
+ lemon zest
+ lychee

KINH GIOI

ELSHOLTZIA CILIATA

Also known as Vietnamese lemon mint, *kinh gioi* is one of those herbs that people try for the first time and immediately regret not having discovered sooner—all because it's so fresh and minty. The serrated, bright green leaves are similar in scent and flavor to lemon verbena and lemongrass. *Kinh gioi* is also a perfect starter plant, as it grows easily in a hydroponic environment.

ORIGIN
Asia

SEED TO SPROUT
14 days

**SEED TO
FIRST HARVEST**
35 days

HARVEST STYLE
Branches (page 56)

CULINARY INSPIRATION

Use a classic mojito recipe, muddling *kinh gioi* instead of mint leaves. Marinate a slice of Asian pear in lemonade and use it to garnish the drink.

FLAVOR AND INGREDIENT PAIRINGS

+ cilantro
+ citrus
+ cucumber
+ curry
+ strawberry

LEMON GEM MARIGOLD

TAGETES TENUIFOLIA 'LEMON GEM'

This plant has delicate, fern-like leaves and shoots out small yellow flowers. The leaves contain a citrus-scented oil that gives them the taste of lemon or orange peel. You can use this to good effect in desserts or in rice or grain dishes that have a mild base flavor.

ORIGIN

South America

SEED TO SPROUT

21 days

**SEED TO
FIRST HARVEST**

42 days

HARVEST STYLE

Stalks (page 57)

CULINARY INSPIRATION

Use the leaves and flowers in place of a lemon or orange twist in a cocktail, for a more subtle, vegetal citrus note. Or, similarly, make a fresher vodka and tonic. Go light on the tonic, add a squeeze of lemon, and then add sprigs and flowers of lemon gem marigold to garnish.

FLAVOR AND INGREDIENT PAIRINGS

+ apricot
+ citrus
+ grape
+ tomato
+ vanilla

RAU RAM

PERSICARIA ODORATA

Raum ram is an aromatic and flavorful leaf, sometimes referred to as Vietnamese or Cambodian mint, even though it isn't part of the mint family at all. Its flavor is similar to cilantro, but with additional cinnamon and citrus notes.

CULINARY INSPIRATION

Rau ram is great in summer rolls. Dip some rice paper wrappers in warm water to moisten them up. Transfer them to a plate and place fillings in the middle: pea shoots, chopped toasted peanuts, fried tofu, thinly sliced carrots, and a generous helping of rau ram leaves. Roll them up and enjoy as a light summer treat.

ORIGIN
Asia

SEED TO SPROUT
Grown from cuttings
(page 60)

**SEED TO
FIRST HARVEST**
Grown from cuttings
(page 60)

FLAVOR AND INGREDIENT PAIRINGS

+   bean sprouts
+   chilis
+   coconut milk
+   noodles
+   peppermint

HARVEST STYLE
Branches (page 56)

RED SHISO

PERILLA FRUTESCENS VAR. CRISPA

This plant sports beautiful purple-red leaves and stems. Also known as red perilla and as beefsteak plant for its color, red shiso has a flavor and aroma similar to that of green shiso, perhaps with a little more anise, so your choice of which one to plant can be based on aesthetic reasons, rather than flavor.

ORIGIN

Asia

SEED TO SPROUT

10 days

**SEED TO
FIRST HARVEST**

31 days

HARVEST STYLE

Branches (page 56)

CULINARY INSPIRATION

Roast a whole cauliflower using your favorite recipe. Meanwhile, make a shiso oil by mincing red shiso leaves and combining them with minced ginger, oil, vinegar, and a touch of sugar or honey. Serve the oil as a dressing with freshly torn red shiso leaves and black sesame seeds, for an aromatic, visually arresting, flavorful combination.

FLAVOR AND INGREDIENT PAIRINGS

+   chive
+   ginger
+   miso
+   mushroom
+   sage

SUCCULENT ICEPLANT

MESEMBRYANTHEMUM CRYSTALLINUM

The iceplant gets its name from the small fibers on the leaf and stem that cause it to sparkle in the light. This is a delicate plant, sensitive to variations in nutrients, light, and heat. But it's worth the effort to grow it. When done successfully, it is visually intriguing and delicious.

ORIGIN
Asia

SEED TO SPROUT
21 days

SEED TO FIRST HARVEST
49 days

HARVEST STYLE
Branches (page 56)

CULINARY INSPIRATION

Since the flavor is subtle, it can help to refresh stronger flavors on the plate. Try it in small, delicate dishes like *amuse-bouches* or dessert. For example, a panna cotta plus berries might include iceplant dipped in a little powdered sugar as garnish.

FLAVOR AND INGREDIENT PAIRINGS

+   black tea
+   fig
+   nut milks
+   sesame oil
+   sesame seed

SWEET THAI BASIL

OCIMUM BASILICUM VAR. THYRSIFLORA

One of the most common varieties of basil, and especially popular in Southeast Asia, sweet Thai basil actually originates in Vietnam. It has a spicy anise flavor and aroma and is best used as a garnish on sweet Thai or other Asian dishes.

ORIGIN
Asia

SEED TO SPROUT
10 days

SEED TO FIRST HARVEST
31 days

HARVEST STYLE
Branches (page 56)

CULINARY INSPIRATION

Toss one-inch chunks of watermelon in rice vinegar, orange juice, and lime juice, and add some sliced cucumber. Add hot sauce to taste. Season with salt and pepper, and garnish with chopped toasted peanuts and a generous amount of torn Thai basil leaves.

FLAVOR AND INGREDIENT PAIRINGS

+ coconut
+ curry
+ ginger
+ peach
+ tomato

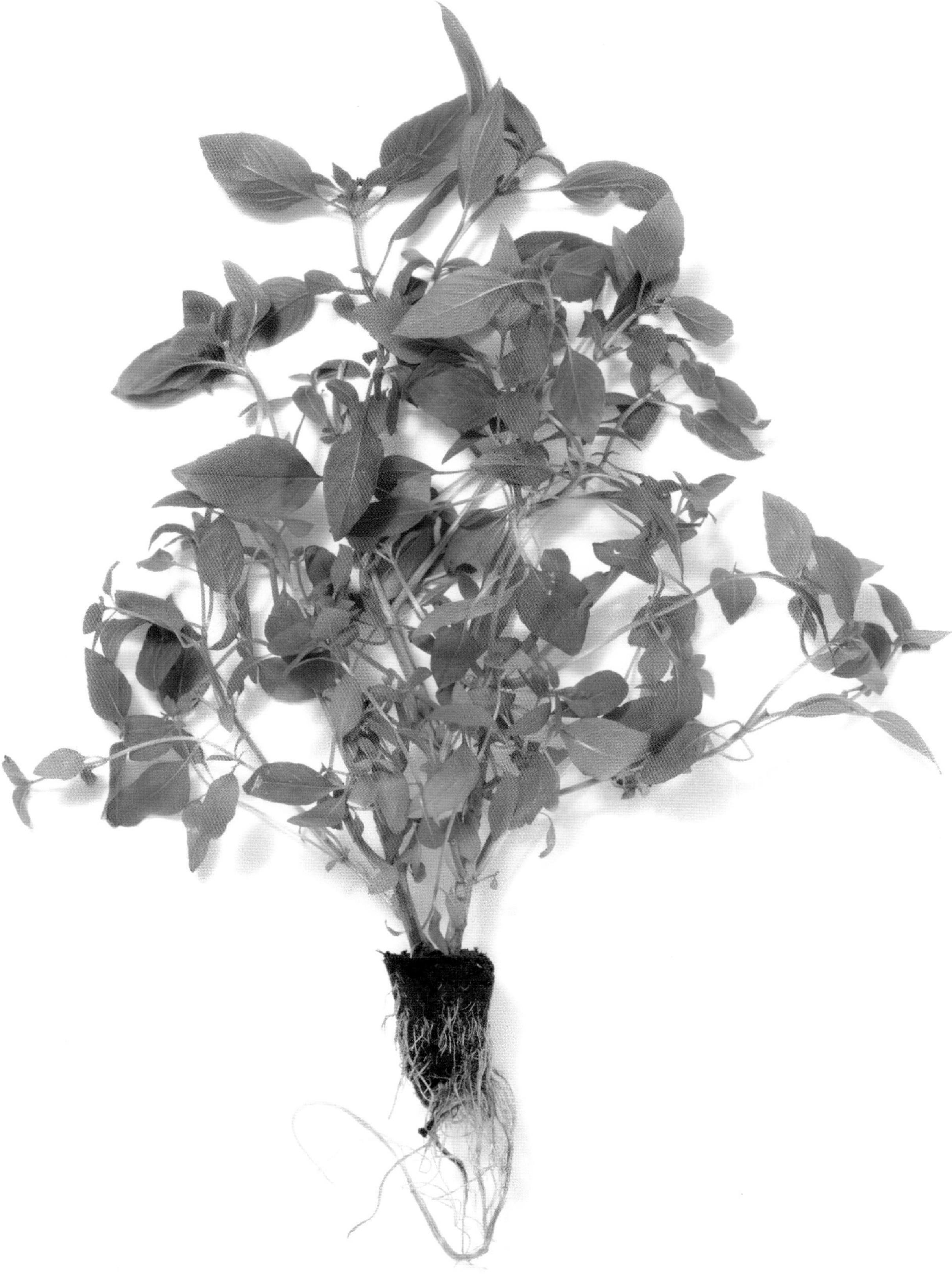

SWEET THAI BASIL

WASABI ARUGULA

DIPLOTAXIS ERUCOIDES

With an intense kick mimicking the flavor of wasabi root, this arugula variety is always a pleasure to serve, as it never fails to surprise guests. Although it is spicy, the flavor is not overwhelming. This plant easily starts to flower, producing small white-yellow blooms, and the flowers are equally delicious.

ORIGIN
Asia

SEED TO SPROUT
21 days

**SEED TO
FIRST HARVEST**
49 days

HARVEST STYLE
Stalks (page 57)

CULINARY INSPIRATION

Season broccolini with olive oil, salt, and pepper and char it on a hot grill (or in a grill pan). Make a quick sauce with tahini, minced garlic, fresh lemon juice, a little warm water, salt, and pepper. Pour over the charred broccolini, then garnish with wasabi arugula leaves and black sesame seeds to add a spicy bite to this summer dish perfect for grilling season.

FLAVOR AND INGREDIENT PAIRINGS

+   apple
+   avocado
+   olive oil
+   plum
+   shiso

GARDEN OF EXOTIC PLANTS

The plants in this section come from all over the world. There's no connection among them apart from the fact that they are unusual and delightful. Some of them, like the toothache plant, are on the edge of what can be considered a culinary plant. Its red-and-yellow buttons (which are actually collections of dozens of miniscule flowers) poke out of lush, dark green foliage. They are part of a cluster, arranged on a stem composed of multiple branches, and are indeed strange looking. If you came across this plant for the first time in its native Amazon, where it is known as *jambu*, you would almost certainly avoid it, as its bold colors suggest danger. The buttons, stems, and leaves can be eaten and deliver a surprising, slowly revealed but long-lasting effect. Some describe it as a numbing sensation. Others taste a grassy note followed by a rush of saliva. Many simply can't find words to explain the feeling, so resort to drooling.

The other plants in this section all have surprising elements in one way or another, making them equally fun to grow at home and share with your friends. And the best part is that they all grow well hydroponically.

AZTEC SWEET HERB

PHYLA DULCIS

An intriguing (and almost confusing) sweet herb with aromas of savory camphor but a sweet, stevia-like flavor. The plant grows with dryish serrated leaves, branches quickly like a mint, and will spread rapidly if left unchecked. Small buttons form, which have a concentrated flavor and sweetness to them.

ORIGIN

North America

SEED TO SPROUT

14 days

SEED TO FIRST HARVEST

21 days

HARVEST STYLE

Hedges (page 58)

CULINARY INSPIRATION

Use the buttons and leaves for sweetness in a quick chopped cantaloupe salad with a little lime, salt, and chile flakes. The herb will intensify the flavors of the melon and add an interesting camphor note. Try with desserts to add a sweet note without sugar.

FLAVOR AND INGREDIENT PAIRINGS

+ anise
+ cheese
+ lemon
+ mint
+ thyme

CHEESE PLANT

RUBIACEAE FAMILY

An unusual strain from Southeast Asia, the cheese plant has a strong cheesy smell that starts the moment you brush or tear the leaves or stem. The plant grows extremely rapidly, with new tendrils popping out all the time and growing inches per day. It is unique and may not be to everyone's liking, but when used sparingly, it can make dishes exciting and unusual.

ORIGIN
Asia

SEED TO SPROUT
10 days

**SEED TO
FIRST HARVEST**
31 days

HARVEST STYLE
Branches (page 56)

CULINARY INSPIRATION

The obvious use of the cheese plant is to bring its funkiness to a vegan cheese plate, such as pairing it with a cashew or almond cheese. You can serve the cheese with torn leaves, or you can mince the leaves and then roll a log of the cheese in a mixture of minced cheese plant and other herbs.

FLAVOR AND INGREDIENT PAIRINGS

+ basil
+ cheese
+ olive oil
+ sage
+ tomato

DRAGON'S TONGUE ARUGULA

DIPLOTAXIS TENUIFOLIA

This arugula variety got its name from the prominent red vein that runs down the center of its leaf. The flavor is generally spicier and more intense than regular arugula, so while the leaves are smaller, they can give a dish a surprising kick. The plant will produce attractive yellow flowers with a similar great taste over time.

CULINARY INSPIRATION

One of the simplest and best ways to serve dragon's tongue arugula is with fresh figs and a little of your favorite cheese, perhaps with a drizzle of honey, some lemon juice, and sea salt.

ORIGIN

Europe

SEED TO SPROUT

21 days

FLAVOR AND INGREDIENT PAIRINGS

+ almond

SEED TO FIRST HARVEST

21 days

+ balsamic vinegar

+ beet

+ peach

HARVEST STYLE

Stalks (page 57)

+ tomato

EPAZOTE

DYSPHANIA AMBROSIOIDES

This robust herb has a particularly strong flavor and aroma, and the more mature the plant becomes, the more pungent the taste, so older leaves should be used sparingly. Epazote is commonly used in Mexican and Caribbean kitchens and especially complements bean dishes.

ORIGIN

Mexico and
South America

SEED TO SPROUT

14 days

**SEED TO
FIRST HARVEST**

35 days

HARVEST STYLE

Stalks (page 57)

CULINARY INSPIRATION

Epazote's perfect match is bean-based dishes, where you can use it dried or fresh. Also try it in places you might use cilantro, and you'll find its minty character adds a refreshing flavor. For example, chop handfuls of epazote leaves and stir them into a sweet potato salad.

FLAVOR AND INGREDIENT PAIRINGS

+ avocado

+ caraway

+ cinnamon

+ coriander

+ oregano

MORINGA

MORINGA OLEIFERA

Moringa's dark, emerald-green leaves are flat and round, unique in their absolutely striking appearance, especially against a pure white plate. They are soft but starchy when eaten, with a vegetal quality and nuttiness. The plant is a tree, and it will grow to forty feet tall if unchecked, but you can keep it small by pruning it continuously.

CULINARY INSPIRATION

Moringa is far more about nutrition than flavor. Add a handful of the leaves to a smoothie for a high vitamin C boost, or include them raw or quickly sautéed in a grain bowl or taco.

ORIGIN

India

SEED TO SPROUT

14 days

FLAVOR AND INGREDIENT PAIRINGS

SEED TO FIRST HARVEST

42 days

+ banana

+ carrot

+ citrus

+ radish

HARVEST STYLE

Branches (page 56)

+ spinach

PÁPALO

POROPHYLLUM RUDERALE

This plant started it all for me. It's like cilantro, but with a stronger, very fresh, almost citrusy and soap-hinted flavor. More crunch. More mintiness. It is often eaten raw as a garnish in central Mexican dishes, especially on *cemitas*, the popular Puebla-style sandwiches of sesame-studded rolls stuffed with a meat of some kind, cheese, onion, and chile.

ORIGIN

North America

SEED TO SPROUT

14 days

SEED TO FIRST HARVEST

42 days

HARVEST STYLE

Branches (page 56)

CULINARY INSPIRATION

Pápalo is traditionally used to cut through the fattiness of Mexican pork and cheese sandwiches, so you can definitely take this approach at home. It's also delicious and special on its own as a garnish for a chocolate pudding dessert or in a light starter, such as ceviche.

FLAVOR AND INGREDIENT PAIRINGS

+   avocado
+   citrus
+   garlic
+   tomatillo
+   tomato

PURPLE OXALIS

OXALIS TRIANGULARIS

Also known as purple shamrock (although the shape differs from a traditional shamrock), purple oxalis is an edible plant related to sorrel. The plant is grown from a rhisome (a subterranean stem). The leaves are deep purple and triangular, and the flowers are a beautiful rich purpley-pink. Both have a high concentration of oxalic acid, which gives it a tangy, sour taste with citrusy overtones. You can use this to balance overly sweet, fatty, or rich dishes without having to add citrus.

ORIGIN
South America

SEED TO SPROUT
10 days

SEED TO FIRST HARVEST
31 days

HARVEST STYLE
Stalks (page 57)

CULINARY INSPIRATION

The enchanting shape and color of the leaves and flowers make them a welcome addition to a wide variety of plates. The sour stems bring a strong citrus note that you can use to break up the creamy, fatty elements in dishes like cheesy pastas or rich, buttery desserts.

FLAVOR AND INGREDIENT PAIRINGS

+ butter
+ cream
+ gruyère
+ parmigiano-reggiano
+ ricotta

TOOTHACHE PLANT

SPILANTHES ACMELLA

When eaten, the buds of this plant create intense sensations in the mouth, which is how the plant got its name and why it's also been dubbed buzz buttons, Szechuan buttons, and electric buttons. At first you'll notice a grassy flavor, which is soon replaced by a prickling and numbing sensation, excessive salivation, and then a cooling feeling in the throat. A concentrated extract of the plant is used as a flavoring agent in many countries and is variously described as having a citrusy, tropical, or musty odor and pungent, tingling, numbing, or effervescent flavor.

ORIGIN
South America

SEED TO SPROUT
14 days

SEED TO FIRST HARVEST
42 days

HARVEST STYLE
Branches (page 56)

CULINARY INSPIRATION

The buttons can be overwhelming (but fun) if used whole. The leaves, on the other hand, allow for a more nuanced approach, allowing you to control the power of the spilanthol (the plant's sensation-causing compound) in a dish. Try tossing a few of the leaves in a simple arugula salad, or blanching the leaves and blending into an herb oil.

FLAVOR AND INGREDIENT PAIRINGS

+ basil
+ custard apple
+ grapefruit peel
+ kimchi
+ lemon zest

YARROW

ACHILLEA MILLEFOLIUM

Yarrow, also known as old man's pepper, soldier's wound wort (because of its healing properties), and nosebleed, can be found in common grassy places and often by the road. Its leaves are considered feathery and are about four inches in length. In early summer, white blooms begin to appear on the plant that are flavorful and attractive. Yarrow is used for numerous medicinal purposes, including fighting kidney infections, curing colds, and strengthening the body. In the kitchen, the somewhat bitter leaves can be used as a garnish, in teas, or to infuse oils.

ORIGIN

North America
and Europe

SEED TO SPROUT

14 days

**SEED TO
FIRST HARVEST**

42 days

HARVEST STYLE

Stalks (page 57)

CULINARY INSPIRATION

Make a yarrow-parsley oil by blanching parsley, then shocking it in a bowl of ice water. Combine with chopped yarrow leaves and a light oil (like canola) in a high-speed blender. The oil is great with roasted vegetables, in cold soups, or in a vinaigrette. You can also use fresh yarrow as a garnish for soft fruit, like very ripe sliced peaches.

FLAVOR AND INGREDIENT PAIRINGS

+   anise hyssop

+   beer

+   cardamom

+   honey

+   licorice

GARDEN OF MICROGREENS

The nuttiness of arugula packed into a tiny, pretty leaf, the bold pink of an amaranth petal—you can see why microgreens are so popular among chefs.

No one's completely sure when and where microgreens first started turning up regularly on dinner plates. It was most likely in San Francisco in the 1980s. There's also no strict USDA definition of a microgreen versus a cress, a sprout, or a baby leaf—all forms that many would argue predated microgreens. Technically, almost any herb or green can be grown as a microgreen. In practice, many varieties are too spindly or weird looking in their awkward childhood phase— ugly ducklings that won't add to a plate's appeal. Many also simply don't have much flavor until they mature, putting them into dangerous nonfunctional garnish territory.

You can plant microgreens in anything that allows them access to moisture, nutrients, air, and some light. Since they do develop roots, you want something porous and thick enough for them to build a little foundation—a popular substrate is rockwool (see page 30). Depending on the variety, many micros are ready to harvest between seven to fourteen days. You should be looking for a healthy mini plant that is two to three inches tall and has developed the leaf structure you want. This could be cotyledons or it could include a number of mature leaves. It depends on the plant and the aesthetic you're going for on the plate.

Some recent studies suggest that microgreens are more nutritious than mature plants. For example, red cabbage microgreens have six times more vitamin C than mature red cabbage of the same weight, and nearly seventy times more vitamin K. The most nutrient-dense micros seem to be red cabbage, cilantro, garnet amaranth, and green daikon radish. Growing broccoli sprouts may be the easiest way to access this kind of nutrient boost. No large-scale epidemiological trials of microgreens have been done to date, however, so it's probably safe to say they are very good for you and leave it at that.

For the home cook, microgreens can be a fun and simple way to add a bit of color to dishes and can help take a dinner party to a more sophisticated level. That's reason enough to try to grow some of your own.

BABY BORAGE

BORAGO OFFICINALIS

Borage has a flavor that evokes cucumber and celery. Its thick leaves provide a great succulent crunch and texture in a dish.

ORIGIN
Europe

SEED TO SPROUT
14 days

**SEED TO
FIRST HARVEST**
21 days

HARVEST STYLE
Microgreens
(page 59)

CULINARY INSPIRATION

Make a simple pea soup by frying scallions and garlic, then add vegetable stock and frozen peas. Purée in a blender until smooth. Garnish with a little grated Parmigiano-Reggiano cheese, if you like, then finish with baby borage leaves and flowers for a cucumber-textured topping for this quick but flavorful dish.

FLAVOR AND INGREDIENT PAIRINGS

+ garlic
+ lemon
+ mint
+ onion
+ tomato

MICRO ARUGULA

ERUCA SATIVA

This microgreen produces heart-shaped leaves with a nutty, peppery flavor. Incredibly popular in salad mixes, micro arugula can also be used as a garnish, best paired with tomatoes, citrus, and Parmesan cheese. Don't underestimate the size: it brings big flavor.

ORIGIN
The Mediterranean

SEED TO SPROUT
14 days

**SEED TO
FIRST HARVEST**
14 days

HARVEST STYLE
Microgreens
(page 59)

CULINARY INSPIRATION

Micro arugula brings a nuttiness and pepperiness to almost any dish, so make it visible. Avocado toast is no fine-dining meal, but with good bread, a ripe avocado, a drizzle of good olive oil, lemon juice, salt and pepper, and micro arugula on top, the dish becomes a special weekend snack or hors d'oeuvre to welcome guests.

FLAVOR AND INGREDIENT PAIRINGS

+   balsamic vinegar
+   beet
+   endive
+   garlic
+   radicchio

MICRO MAGENTA SPREEN

CHENOPODIUM GIGANTEUM

This nutritious plant, rich in vitamins A and C, calcium, and iron, comes from the same family as spinach, chard, and beets but has a milder flavor profile. It gets its name from the splash of hot magenta pink at the top of each stem. It is one of the many chenopods, or lamb's quarters, that have a long history of being grown in gardens or gathered wild.

ORIGIN

India

SEED TO SPROUT

14 days

**SEED TO
FIRST HARVEST**

21 days

HARVEST STYLE

Microgreens
(page 59)

CULINARY INSPIRATION

Since its flavor is mild, magenta spreen is best used for its appearance. The magenta and green coloring goes beautifully with purple foods like purple potatoes or eggplant. Slice a Japanese eggplant in half lengthwise, salt the cut sides, and let it sit for a half hour until the moisture is drawn out, then wipe it off, rub with a generous amount of olive oil and garlic, and roast at around 400°F for 30 to 40 minutes. Finish with a sprinkling of vibrant magenta spreen tops.

FLAVOR AND INGREDIENT PAIRINGS

+ chiles

+ egg

+ feta

+ mustard greens

+ spinach

MICRO RED AMARANTH

AMARANTHUS CRUENTUS

This showy plant boasts a beautiful magenta color throughout oval leaves and its stem. The plant has a dry, earthy flavor, which mixes well with other micros. It's often chosen by chefs for its incredibly unique color and appearance.

ORIGIN
South America

SEED TO SPROUT
14 days

SEED TO FIRST HARVEST
14 days

HARVEST STYLE
Microgreens
(page 59)

CULINARY INSPIRATION

Use the color of these delicate little leaves to make a roast onion dish special. Slice red onions vertically almost all the way through and let each one spread out into a star shape. Season them with olive oil, minced garlic, cumin, and chile slices. Roast at 350°F for about 45 minutes, or until tender. To serve, sprinkle with cut red amaranth leaves for a beautiful color and taste combination.

FLAVOR AND INGREDIENT PAIRINGS

+ basil
+ eggs
+ garlic
+ seafood
+ tomato

PEA TENDRILS

PISUM SATIVUM

Pea tendrils and shoots bring fresh summer pea taste in a delicate, beautiful form on the plate. They work especially well in spring and summer dishes when their light flavor and color complement the season's bounty.

ORIGIN
Europe

SEED TO SPROUT
14 days

SEED TO FIRST HARVEST
16 days

HARVEST STYLE
Microgreens
(page 59)

CULINARY INSPIRATION

Pea tendrils are so pretty that it would be a shame to lose them in a complex dish. An easy way to be sure they shine is to make a simple pasta. Boil some pasta, and in the meantime, sauté a minced clove of garlic in olive oil. Drain the pasta, add to the skillet, and stir in a handful of thumb-size pea tendril pieces until they wilt slightly and the pasta is well coated. Season with salt, pepper, and chopped mint.

FLAVOR AND INGREDIENT PAIRINGS

+ carrot
+ gin
+ potato
+ vanilla
+ white chocolate

RUBY STREAKS MUSTARD

BRASSICA JUNCEA

This micro has a slightly spicy flavor packed into purple-tinged leaves. The young leaves are round, and the more mature leaves are frilly.

CULINARY INSPIRATION

The delicate mustard flavor and crunch of the stems is simple and spicy, so no need to reinvent the wheel here: serve fresh in a simple salad with cherry tomatoes and a light vinaigrette.

ORIGIN
Europe

SEED TO SPROUT
14 days

FLAVOR AND INGREDIENT PAIRINGS

+ cheddar
+ cream
+ sour cream
+ strawberry
+ yogurt

SEED TO FIRST HARVEST
14 days

HARVEST STYLE
Microgreens
(page 59)

GARDEN OF EXPERIMENTATION

Some of the most interesting plants you can grow are new, unique varieties of common plants that can be created through simple selection techniques. There's an entire cottage industry of home growers doing this, and you should try it, too, as it gives you the opportunity to tailor the plant to your own taste.

To start, you'll need to identify a special, unique characteristic of a plant that you find particularly desirable. Maybe it's a strong flavor, an unexpected aroma, or an uncommon appearance. It can be anything that sets the specimen apart from the regular plant variety. Once you have a plant whose feature you wish to replicate, you have two choices. You can grow the plant out until it starts flowering and creating seeds, and then plant those seeds and aim to identify the same, hopefully intensified characteristic in the next generation. Alternatively, you can take cuttings from the original plant (also called a "sport") and replicate the plant from the cuttings. Keep in mind, however, that plants grown from seeds of cuttings may not continue to display the same characteristic.

Because these two methods have been applied over time, we now have dozens of varieties of popular herbs like mint and basil. Many of them can only be grown from cuttings, however, which means you can buy them as live plants, not as seeds. This is not a huge problem, as you can take cuttings from the plant and root them in your system, or you can unpack some of the soil from the live plant and repack it with a hydroponic growth medium.

In this section, I'll show you some of the most interesting examples of mint and basil plants I've come across. You'll be surprised how different some of them are in their appearance and flavor, so much so that it's tough to recognize them as the original plant.

BERRIES AND CREAM MINT

MENTHA 'BERRIES AND CREAM'

This mint has dark green, smallish leaves, a somewhat fruity mint aroma, and an unusual taste. It doesn't taste exactly like berries and cream, but works well in summer drinks.

BLUE SPICE BASIL

OCIMUM BASILICUM

Prized for its floral sweetness with a hint of vanilla, this attractive basil produces a dense column of purple flowers when at peak maturity. Its leaves are great in fruit salads or as a seasoning in poultry dishes.

CHOCOLATE MINT

MENTHA × PIPERITA 'CHOCOLATE'

This mint variety looks similar to generic mint, except it often has a browner, deep burgundy–colored stem. Its flavor offers subtle notes of cocoa, and it is commonly used in desserts and as a garnish for cocktails.

CITRUS KITCHEN MINT

MENTHA 'UTILITY CITRUS KITCHEN'

Although similar in appearance to peppermint, this variety has a slightly lemony, citrusy aspect, making it perfect for drinks and desserts.

GRAPEFRUIT MINT

MENTHA × PIPERITA 'GRAPEFRUIT'

The slightly furry, deep-green leaves of this hearty mint have a flavor that recalls the plant's namesake fruit: a slightly bitter taste with a citrusy character.

LEMON BASIL

OCIMUM BASILICUM VAR. CITRIODORA

This basil variety has a sweet, lemony flavor and fragrance. A popular addition to Indonesian and Thai dishes, it's delicious in stir-fries, soups, and curries. Be careful not to overcook it, as its flavor will disappear.

MARSHMALLOW MINT

MENTHA 'MARSHMALLOW'

Jim Westerfield, the creator of this mint and many others in this section, has described this plant's aroma as "the first marshmallow out of the bag." The mix of the smell of marshmallow and the flavor of mint is both unusual and surprisingly appealing.

MOUNTAIN MINT

PYCNANTHEMUM VERTICILLATUM VAR. PILOSUM

Mountain mint has thinner, longer, darker leaves than more commonly used mints and a strong, almost spicy aroma when crushed. It's often used in teas and fragrant sauces.

PINK CANDYPOPS MINT

MENTHA 'PINK CANDYPOPS'

This mint is so named because, unlike the elongated blooms of regular mint, it produces flowers shaped like lollipops. It boasts an unusual aroma as well, which is a little like an herb butter.

PLUTO BASIL

OCIMUM BASILICUM 'PLUTO'

One of my favorite varieties to grow and taste, this is a dwarf basil with dark green leaves. It produces a fine basil flavor and aroma with a touch of mint. Incredibly branched and compact, the stems are easily chewed, making it possible to plate whole bunches.

PURPLE AMETHYST BASIL

OCIMUM BASILICUM 'AMETHYST IMPROVED'

This variation on basil has thick, deep purple leaves. Both the leaves and flowers of this annual plant are edible and are the perfect garnish for cocktails, salads, soups, and desserts, imparting a pungent basil flavor with more anise notes than the common Genovese basil.

INTO THE FUTURE

Discovering so many unknown, forgotten, or out-of-reach plants has been a true journey, one which I hope to continue my whole life. I'm also enthusiastic about the future made possible by hydroponics and indoor farming because of all the other great benefits it can bring. We can reduce our food miles by growing food hyperlocally, which in turn reduces the need for packaging and makes food waste less likely. We can save water with hydroponics, making it possible to grow fresh food in drought-prone areas. And we can get closer to our food by building farms in our cities in unused or unrentable spaces. With the price of LEDs continually decreasing, building indoor farms can be affordable, giving communities more power to grow their own food.

One of the most enjoyable things I do at Farm.One is to encourage young people to try their first fresh herb, straight off the plant. We have many kids who come and visit who are clearly more comfortable picking up a chicken nugget than a fresh leaf. Their experience at the farm shows them how exciting plants are and how accessible real food production can be if we bring it into our cities. I like to think that a new generation of food connoisseurs can be created by bringing agriculture closer to the community in this way. I'm excited about these approaches becoming more prevalent.

We are also now reaching a stage with technology where we can put farms in all kinds of previously unthinkable places, including cruise ships, oil rigs, military vessels, remote islands, Arctic research stations—even space. While they will provide only a portion of the food requirements in these situations, they will make fresh and undeniably healthy food available and attractive year-round, hopefully making greens and herbs the primary choice for more and more people, rather than relegating them to a side dish as often happens in the standard American diet.

Food is, and probably always will be, a serious, complex problem for developed and developing nations. Part of our current dilemma is that by industrializing large-scale agriculture we have distanced ourselves from food production and lost our understanding about plants, our access to diversity, and our contact with simple, whole plant food. Hydroponics and indoor farming now give us an opportunity to reclaim all these things, while also having lots of fun and eating some delicious, surprising, exciting plants.

RESOURCES

SEED SOURCES

Baker Creek Heirloom Seeds
rareseeds.com

Kitazawa Seed Company
kitazawaseed.com

Johnny's Selected Seeds
johnnyseeds.com

Stokes Seeds
stokeseeds.com

OFF-THE-SHELF HYDROPONIC SYSTEMS

+Farm
plus.farm

HAMAMA
hamama.cc

AeroGarden
aerogarden.com

Sprouts IO
sprouts.io

AVA
avagrows.com

Tower Garden
towergarden.com

Click & Grow
clickandgrow.com

Urban Leaf
geturbanleaf.com

Cloud Farms
cloud-farms.com

BRICK-AND-MORTAR STORES FOR HYDROPONIC SUPPLIES

Chicago Roots Hydroponics and Organics

4020 West Irving Park Road

Chicago, IL 60641

773.545.4020

chicagorootshydro.com

GreenCoast Hydroponics

13 locations: Downtown Los Angeles, Escondido, Hesperia, Los Angeles International Airport, Long Beach, Ontario, Orange, Santa Barbara, Temecula, Van Nuys, and Venice, California; Las Vegas, Nevada; Portland, Oregon

gchydro.com

The Grow Room

32–32 49th Street

Astoria, NY 11103

718.545.4769

8 Bridge Street

Nyack, NY 10960

845.348.8811

thegrowroom.com

LIHYDRO

3104 Expressway Drive South

Islandia, NY 11749

631.651.8281

lihydro.com

BOOKS

Boyle, Robert. *The Sceptical Chymist: The Classic 1661 Text.* Mineola, NY: Dover Publications, 2003.

Page, Karen. *The Flavor Bible: The Essential Guide to Culinary Creativity, Based on the Wisdom of America's Most Imaginative Chefs.* New York: Little, Brown and Company, 2008.

Page, Karen. *The Flavor Bible: The Essential Guide to Culinary Creativity with Vegetables, Fruits, Grains, Legumes, Nuts, Seeds, and More, Based on the Wisdom of Leading American Chefs.* New York: Little, Brown and Company, 2008.

ACKNOWLEDGMENTS

A huge thank you to everyone who has supported me: the whole team at Farm.One, for working so hard and joining me on this crazy mission. Henry Gordon-Smith and the whole team at Blue Planet Consulting for their valuable guidance. All our customers, large and small, because this would not be possible without you.

My family, for entertaining my unusual ideas on the other side of the world.

David Dietz, Chok Ooi, Felix Miller, Christophe Fraise, and John Cassidy for their valuable support early on.

Ronny, Jill, Jodi, and the team at Atera for warmly welcoming us into their home.

Richard and the team at ICE—I don't think you knew what you were getting yourselves into!

And finally, the farmer who first gave me pápalo, for kicking off a journey of discovery.

ABOUT THE AUTHOR

Rob Laing is the CEO and founder of Farm.One, an indoor hydroponic farm in Manhattan. Started in 2016, Farm.One grows rare herbs, edible flowers, microgreens, and other exotic, pesticide-free plants year-round. Produce grown at Farm.One is used by some of New York City's finest restaurants.

Rob is an experienced startup founder who is passionate about plant-based eating and using technology for clean, accessible food. Rob grew up in London and Melbourne, and has lived in Hong Kong, Brussels, and Tokyo. A former designer, he has a BA from University of the Arts, London.

INDEX

DOVETAIL

Text copyright © 2018 by Rob Laing
Photographs copyright © 2018 by Scott Gordon Bleicher
Design by Justin Fuller

Published by Dovetail Press in Brooklyn, New York, a division of Assembly Brands LLC.

For details or ordering information, contact the publisher at the address below or email
info@dovetail.press.

Dovetail Press
42 West Street #403
Brooklyn, NY 11222
www.dovetail.press

Library of Congress Cataloging-in-Publication data is on file with the publisher.
ISBN: 978-0-99873-996-0
First printing, March 2018
Printed in China
10 9 8 7 6 5 4 3 2 1